Alternative Routes to Teaching

ALTERNATIVE ROUTES TO TEACHING

Mapping the New Landscape
of Teacher Education

EDITED BY

PAM GROSSMAN AND SUSANNA LOEB

HARVARD EDUCATION PRESS
CAMBRIDGE, MASSACHUSETTS

Library of Congress Control Number 2008928882

Paperback ISBN 978-1-934742-00-6
Library Edition ISBN 978-1-934742-01-3

Published by Harvard Education Press,
an imprint of the Harvard Education Publishing Group

Harvard Education Press
8 Story Street
Cambridge, MA 02138

Cover Design: Nancy Goulet/studio;wink

The typefaces used in this book are Adobe Garamond Pro for text and Hypatia Sans Pro for display.

To David Kahn and Steve Pokorny,
who waited patiently for the work to end
so we could all go outside

Contents

Introduction

Pam Grossman and Susanna Loeb

Over the past two decades, alternative routes into teaching have become a pervasive feature of the teacher-education landscape. While alternative routes were relatively rare in the 1980s, virtually all states now allow some form of alternative certification; some states, such as Florida, require districts to provide for alternative routes into teaching. In certain states, such as New Jersey and California, alternative certification is one of the primary routes through which new teachers enter the classroom; for example, roughly 40 percent of New Jersey's teachers enter the field of education through alternative routes.[1] In other states, including Alaska, Washington, Vermont, and North Dakota, relatively few teachers complete alternative routes.[2]

Despite its ubiquity, the value of alternative certification has been hotly debated. Some argue that the existence of alternative routes will lead to the de-professionalization of teaching, while others argue that alternative certification represents a better alternative to traditional teacher education.[3] While in the past few years, there have been an increasing number of studies focused on alternative certification, such studies have generated more heat than light with regard to the value of alternative certification or its role in addressing issues of teacher quality. In this volume we attempt to provide a dispassionate review of the evidence on alternative certification, drawing on the research from the late 1980s through the present. Our goal is to move beyond the simple dichotomies that have characterized the debate and begin to look carefully at the trade-offs implicit in any route into teaching.

For example, the existence of alternative certification has demonstrated that we can attract a different pool of candidates into teaching; most research suggests that alternative routes are generally able to attract a more diverse pool of prospective teachers, with regard to both race and gender, who may also have stronger academic qualifications. In looking at alternative certification programs that attract teachers with stronger academic qualifications, we might ask to what extent these kinds of characteristics compensate for the more limited professional course work and restricted field experiences that may also characterize such programs. The research also clearly illustrates that most teachers who enter through alternative routes are teaching in urban schools; there are few teachers from alternative routes teaching in Scarsdale, New York, or Beverly Hills, California. Given that high-poverty urban schools are more likely to have teachers with lower academic qualifications,[4] recruiting teachers from alternative routes may actually improve the profile of those teaching in the most high-poverty schools.[5] At the same time, we may question whether policies that send teachers with more limited preparation to the most challenging schools truly serve the students in these schools.

As indicated in chapter 6, "Assessing the Effectiveness of Teachers from Different Pathways: Issues and Results," the evidence on how teachers from alternative routes perform in classrooms is mixed, suggesting that the existence of alternative certification

2

alone cannot solve the problem of attracting and retaining higher-quality teachers. We argue that a solution to the problem of teacher quality may lie in taking the best innovations of alternative routes, particularly with regard to recruitment and selection of a talented and diverse pool of candidates, and marrying that with stronger preparation and support for new teachers.

The rapid growth of alternative-route programs has also demonstrated the need for institutions that prepare teachers to be more responsive to the immediate needs of school districts. Alternative routes developed, in large part, because existing institutions could not respond quickly enough to projected and actual teacher shortages, especially in high-need areas. In our conclusion, we take up this issue of responsiveness to local needs, and what we can learn from both research and practice to help teacher-education providers of all stripes address these needs.

HISTORY OF ALTERNATIVE ROUTES INTO TEACHING

The existence of multiple pathways into teaching is not a new phenomenon; for much of our history, teachers were prepared locally, through normal schools and programs run by school districts.[6] However, by the second half of the twentieth century, the vast majority of teachers completed college- or university-based programs of teacher preparation. Concern over teacher shortages in the 1980s sparked interest in creating programs that streamlined entry into teaching, particularly in shortage areas such as math and science and in urban school districts. New Jersey was one of the earliest states to embrace alternative certification in the 1980s through its creation of the Provisional Teacher Certificate in 1985; Los Angeles was one of the first school districts to develop its own internship program.[7] Many of the earliest research studies on alternative certification focused on these two initiatives.[8]

Since 1985, the number of teachers prepared through alternative certification programs has grown exponentially. In 1985, only 275 teachers were prepared through alternative certification programs; in 1995, the number had jumped to 6,932, and in 2005, that number increased almost tenfold to 59,000.[9] The number of states offering alternative certification programs has also increased dramatically. According to the latest counts, between 47 and 50 states allow for some form of alternative certification, although state policies differ in how they define and support such programs; approximately one out of every five teachers is prepared through such a pathway.[10] As mentioned above, this statistic varies dramatically by state.

DEFINITIONAL DILEMMAS AND METHODOLOGICAL CHALLENGES

From its outset, research on alternative certification programs has had to contend with the difficulty of defining what counts as alternative certification and with disentangling the effects of particular pathways from the characteristics of the teachers and the schools in which they teach. Both of these challenges have made research on alternative certification programs difficult to interpret.

The traditional definition of *alternative route* is any pathway into teaching other than the traditional, college- or university-based four-year teacher-preparation program.[11] However, this broad definition would include all of the teacher-preparation programs in the state of California, which by law, are only offered at the postbaccalaureate level. This definition also includes the five-year and fifth-year programs run by many university-based teacher educators around the country, many of whom would be surprised to discover that their programs are being labeled as "alternative." Other definitions focus more on the providers than on the length of programs, stipulating that alternative programs are generally offered by districts, while traditional programs are the province of the university.[12] This definition fails to recognize that most district-run programs partner with colleges and universities to provide course work and supervision. In fact, institutions of higher education are among the largest providers of alternatively certified teachers, leading some to question how alternative such programs might be.[13] The lack of a common definition of alternative certification has plagued both research and public discourse on this topic.

In addition to the labeling problem, research on alternative certification has suffered from the difficulty of disentangling the impact of "pathway" from the impact of "teacher characteristics," or the contexts in which teachers from different pathways teach. Because teachers in some alternative certification programs are more likely to teach in higher-poverty schools with lower-achieving students, comparisons of the impact of teachers from different pathways may confound pathway with characteristics of their students and the schools in which they work.[14] Similar problems have plagued research on teacher retention, since schools with greater percentages of students who live in poverty also have the highest rates of teacher attrition. If researchers do not control for school characteristics, they may attribute differences in retention rates to pathways that are more attributable to differences in school contexts.[15]

However we label or study them, alternative routes are now a seemingly omnipresent feature of the broad landscape of teacher education and play a major role in preparing teachers, alongside college-recommending programs. Despite the pervasiveness of alternative routes, most researchers now agree that the label of "alternative" says little about how teachers are actually recruited and prepared. Multiple large-scale studies comparing alternative and university-based routes confirm that tremendous variation exists within these broad pathways.[16] One of the goals of this volume is to bring some clarity to how we might categorize the differences among these programs and how such differences impact both teacher retention and student achievement.

The proliferation of alternative routes has also shifted the debate from the question of whether such routes into teaching should exist at all to how best to design *all* forms of teacher preparation to better prepare teachers to raise student achievement. In this volume, we focus on what we can learn from the research on alternative certification to improve the quality of teachers and teaching in our schools. While there may not be one best way to prepare teachers, all current forms of preparation could be substantially improved with better evidence of the characteristics of teacher education that have the greatest impact on novice teachers' teaching ability and impact on student learning.

OVERVIEW OF VOLUME

This volume is organized into two distinct sections. The first section addresses what we currently know about the history and characteristics of alternative certification, including characteristics of both the teacher candidates and programs they attend. In chapter 1, "The Development of Alternative Certification Policies and Programs in the United States," Kenneth Zeichner and Elizabeth Hutchinson discuss the development of alternative certification programs, focusing particularly on the rapid growth of these programs and the policy problems they are presumably designed to address. The authors also explore the relatively rapid increase in the number of for-profit providers of teacher-preparation programs. Their chapter reminds us that what we now call "alternative" was once the most common way of preparing teachers for American schools.

Building upon this history, in chapter 2, "Who Goes into Early-Entry Programs?" Karen Hammerness and Michelle Reininger delve into what we know about the characteristics of those who enter alternative certification programs and how participants differ from those in more-traditional programs. They compare teachers from these different pathways into teaching in terms of academic background, age, race/ethnicity, and the factors that led them to consider an alternative route into teaching. The authors also address how the existence of alternative certification programs has affected teacher supply, particularly in difficult-to-staff areas. The authors conclude that while alternative routes in general have succeeded in attracting a more diverse pool of teachers with stronger academic backgrounds into the classroom, not all programs fit this pattern. In looking at recruitment issues, Hammerness and Reininger also consider the implications of new research that illustrates teachers' preference for teaching close to home.

In addition to understanding the candidates who enter teaching through alternative routes, we also need a clearer understanding of program characteristics and variation across programs. In chapter 3, "Getting Beyond the Label: What Characterizes Alternative Certification Programs?" Daniel Humphrey and Marjorie Wechsler provide an overview of what we know about the actual structure and content of alternative certification programs, based on their three-year study of seven programs. They detail variations in program duration, field experience, course work, school context, mentoring among these seven programs, as well as differences in background characteristics of teachers in these programs. The authors also address the extent to which there are enough commonalities across programs for the label of "alternative certification" to be meaningful. The chapter highlights both the diversity of programs that fall into the category of alternative certification, as well as some common structures or approaches. The authors conclude with a discussion of the factors that shape the development of new teachers and argue for a definition of "pathway" that accounts for these factors.

The second part of the book looks at evidence regarding outcomes of alternative certification programs. The chapters in this section look at three different kinds of outcomes: candidates' experiences in these programs; their retention in schools, relative to teachers from other pathways; and their impact on student achievement, relative to teachers who come through more-traditional programs.

In chapter 4, "Is Fast-Track Preparation Enough? It Depends," Susan Moore Johnson and Sarah Birkeland explore the question of what new teachers experience in these programs. They argue that the way teacher candidates experience alternative certification programs is a function of the individual characteristics of each participant; features of the programs themselves; and, finally, the particular school context in which they first teach. Arguing that each program is experienced differently by participants with different profiles, the authors illustrate how new teachers from the same program might succeed or fail, depending upon their own backgrounds and the schools in which they're placed. The chapter echoes the findings of chapter 3 and highlights the importance of looking at issues such as the kind of support teachers in these programs receive, both from the program and from the schools in which they work. The authors also note the importance of matching both programmatic content and ongoing support to characteristics of participants in these programs.

One of the concerns that Johnson and Birkeland raise is the challenge of retaining teachers who do not receive adequate support in their first year of teaching. In chapter 5, "But Do They Stay? Addressing Issues of Teacher Retention through Alternative Certification," Jason Grissom addresses one of the key issues driving the demand for teachers: the relationship between teacher supply and teacher retention. One of the arguments against alternative certification has been the fear that teachers who enter through these pathways will not remain in teaching for more than a few years.[17]

This chapter provides a review of the research on the relationship between alternative certification and teacher retention, identifying factors that contribute to better retention outcomes for teachers. In addition, the chapter explores how alternative certification programs can affect the problem of teacher sorting and inequality—in which teachers with the least qualifications end up teaching in the highest-poverty schools. Finally, Grissom illustrates the danger of ignoring working conditions through analyses of teacher retention through a new examination of 2003–04 Schools and Staffing Survey (SASS) and the 2004–05 Teacher Follow-Up Survey (TFS). Grissom finds that while teachers holding alternative certifications are more likely to leave their positions than are teachers with regular certification, this difference is primarily due to differences in the characteristics of the schools in which they teach. His chapter also details some of the methodological challenges entailed in using large-scale databases, such as SASS, to conduct research on alternative certification.

Ultimately, policymakers want to know what kind of impact alternative certification programs will have on student achievement. There have been a number of recent studies that attempt to compare the achievement of students taught by teachers who enter teaching through different routes.[18] In chapter 6, "Assessing the Effectiveness of Teachers from Different Pathways: Issues and Results," Marsha Ing and Susanna Loeb provide an overview of what we know about the impact of teachers in alternative certification programs on student achievement. The research that looks at student achievement is relatively sparse, with the majority of studies focused on a single program, Teach For America. Loeb and Ing conclude that although the research is too limited to provide clear directions for policymakers, it does suggest the value of recruiting secondary teachers with strong content knowledge, while at the same time pointing to the potential importance of other types of knowledge—perhaps pedagogical knowledge or an understanding of child development—particularly for elementary teachers. The chapter ends with recommendations for how to target the use of alternative certification programs to best support student achievement.

The conclusion, "Taking Stock: Future Directions for Practice and Research," builds on previous chapters in proposing future directions for policy and practice in alternative certification. We return to the place and purpose of alternative certification in the broader landscape of teacher preparation, and discuss to what extent such programs have achieved their goals with regard to: increasing the pool of academically talented teachers; increasing the diversity of the teaching force; and having a positive impact on student achievement, particularly in difficult-to-staff schools. Drawing on earlier chapters, we suggest a different way of categorizing alternative certification programs by looking at a range of factors, including:

• the provider;
• the focus of recruitment efforts;
• labor market needs; and
• the timing and focus of preparation and ongoing support.

We argue for creating a typology based on these factors and then conducting more-systematic studies of how programs with different profiles affect outcomes for teachers and students as a direction for future research in this area. We also look at unintended consequences related to issues of teacher sorting and differential access to quality teachers. Finally, we explore how we can take advantage of what we've learned, particularly with regard to recruitment and selection of teachers, and how we can use this knowledge to strengthen teacher quality and teacher preparation across different routes into teaching.

Another Grossman, in a famous misquote of H. L. Mencken, proclaimed: "Complex problems have simple, easy-to-understand wrong answers." As we hope to demonstrate in this volume, despite its success in recruiting a more diverse, often more academically strong, pool of teachers into the classroom, alternative certification alone is not a simple answer to the complex problem of providing well-qualified teachers for all of our nation's schools. Instead, there are a series of tensions and trade-offs that result from the need to recruit, prepare, and retain an enormous number of teachers each year. The question is not whether or not alternative certification programs are a viable alternative to more-traditional programs overseen by institutions of higher education. Rather, the question is how best to recruit a talented pool of prospective teachers and then develop ways to adequately prepare them for the complex work of classroom teaching.

We would like to acknowledge our colleagues, Don Boyd, Hamp Lankford, and Jim Wyckoff, who have been our partners in our research on pathways into teaching. We would also like to acknowledge the help of Marsha Ing, Rita Simpson-Vlach, and Carol Smith, who provided invaluable help in the preparation of the manuscript. We especially want to thank Carol for her invariably cheerful, professional, and timely help throughout the final process. We would also like to thank our editor, Caroline Chauncey, for her enthusiastic support of this book. Finally, Pam Grossman would like to acknowledge the support of the Center for Advanced Study of the Behavioral Sciences, where this book began.

PART I

History and Characteristics of Alternative Certification Programs

CHAPTER 1

The Development of Alternative Certification Policies and Programs in the United States

Kenneth Zeichner and Elizabeth A. Hutchinson

Throughout the history of formal teacher education in the U.S., a variety of pathways into teaching have existed, both inside and outside colleges and universities.[1] At one time or another since the mid-nineteenth century, seminaries, high schools, academies, normal schools, teacher institutes, county training schools, teachers colleges, community colleges, and colleges and universities have all played important roles in educating the nation's teachers. Fraser argues that throughout much of the nation's history, "most teachers came through what might now be labeled as alternative routes."[2] This included a substantial number of teachers who were prepared in school district–based preservice programs. Fraser notes that "by 1914 virtually every city in the United States with a population of 300,000 or more and 80 percent of those over 100,000 maintained their own teacher preparation program as part of the public school system."[3]

When one examines the history of teacher education in the U.S., it is only for a relatively brief period of time (approximately 1960 through 1990) that colleges and universities held a virtual monopoly over preservice teacher education. Since the early 1980s, there has been an increase in noncollege and nonuniversity routes into teaching, including many new for-profit programs,[4] and more and more teachers are entering teaching through these routes—sometimes with little or no preparation before assuming full responsibility for a classroom.[5] Despite the growth in these alternative programs, overall, most teachers in the U.S. still enter teaching through four-year, five-year, and fifth-year college- and university-based programs. In some parts of the country, though, nearly as many teachers enter the field through routes other than those based at colleges and universities.[6]

The history of teacher certification in the U.S. involves a shift over time from certifying teachers based solely on the basis of interviews and examinations conducted at the local level to an increased reliance on professional education credentials and state oversight of the teacher-education process. As Sedlak concludes: "The practice of bestowing certificates to candidates on the basis of professional education rather than examinations exclusively was dramatically expanded. Whether through examination or educational attainment, certification was becoming centralized at the state level."[7]

Current calls for a market-driven, competitive system of teacher certification (discussed below) would create more alternative routes and would shift control of the certification process largely back to the local level (i.e., school principals). At the same time, such a system would reduce or even eliminate professional education requirements in favor of increased reliance on examinations.[8] This "client-centered" approach to teacher certification is similar to the model that was dominant in the U.S. until about the time of World War I.[9]

DEFINING "ALTERNATIVE" ROUTES TO TEACHING

It is no simple matter to locate and examine alternative certification within the more general and inclusive framework of teacher preparation. The concept of alternative certification suffers two liabilities at the moment. Its meaning is obscure and its forms of implementation are many.[10]

There has been a lot of confusion over the years about what distinguishes an alternative route to teaching from a traditional preservice program. The most common definition of an *alternative route* is anything other than a four- or five-year undergraduate program in a college or university, a definition that classifies college and university postbaccalaureate teacher-preparation programs as alternative.[11] Using this definition, Feistritzer estimates that about one-half of alternative certification programs as defined by the states are run by institutions of higher education (IHEs), and even those that are not, often hire IHE faculty and staff to teach. Walsh and Jacobs's study of forty-nine alternative programs in eleven states supports Feistritzer's conclusions about the heavy involvement of IHEs in what is called alternative certification.[12]

Although college- and university-based postbaccalaureate teacher-preparation programs have been considered alternative routes to teaching by researchers and by those who have tabulated state policies,[13] they have existed for many years in colleges and universities. For example, Harvard University initiated its widely influential Master of Arts in Teaching program in 1936,[14] and for many years California has required at least five years of preparation for secondary teachers[15] and for elementary teachers.[16] Then, following the influence of the Holmes Group, the Carnegie Forum on Education and the Economy, and the American Association of Colleges for Teacher Education,[17] even more universities began to offer teacher-education programs at the postbaccalaureate level.

A national survey of teacher-education institutions in the U.S. in 1999 revealed that about 30 percent of individuals studying to be teachers did so after having received at least a bachelor's degree. About two-thirds of the institutions surveyed reported that they had at least one program for the initial preparation of teachers in which candidates enter at the postbaccalaureate level.[18] It is likely that the number of individuals preparing to teach at the post-baccalaureate level is much higher today than in 1999, given the increased alternatives now available to prospective teachers at the postbaccalaureate level.[19]

For the purposes of this chapter we will adopt the dominant definition of alternative route to teaching that considers college- and university-based postbaccalaureate programs alternative because of how state policies have been tracked and how information was made available to us. It makes more sense, however, in our view, to adopt Boyd et al.'s distinction between programs where the majority of preparation is completed prior to student teaching ("college-recommending") and programs where most of the preparation occurs on the job as a teacher of record ("early-entry").[20] Research on the impact of different pathways into teaching has shown that the level of preparation a teacher has had prior to assuming responsibility for a classroom makes a difference in the quality of teaching during a teacher's first year.[21]

Stoddart and Floden note that advocates of alternative certification believe that individuals who have subject-matter expertise can learn to teach on the job provided they are given adequate professional development and support. Hawley refers to this rationale for alternative routes as the "arts and craft" position, which sees teaching largely as an intuitive craft that can best be learned on the job from other teachers. This view contrasts with the position of many advocates of traditional college and university programs who have argued that teachers must acquire a substantial amount of knowledge and skills before they are ready to begin teaching. Stoddart and Floden argue that what is involved in this debate are different assumptions about what it means to learn to teach and what one needs to learn, not whether someone needs to learn anything to teach.[22]

The choice between a traditional program and an alternative route is not a choice between *some* professional preparation and *no* such preparation, but rather a decision about the timing and institutional context for teacher preparation and the mix of professional knowledge and skills to be acquired.

REASONS FOR THE EMERGENCE OF ALTERNATIVE ROUTES TO TEACHER CERTIFICATION

In addition to the arts-and-craft rationale discussed above, there are a number of reasons why alternative routes into teaching reemerged in the U.S. during the 1980s and have now become a significant aspect of American teacher education.[23] The factor most often cited as the reason for states establishing alternative routes into teaching has been the need to fill teaching vacancies in critical shortage areas. These include real or projected shortages both in particular subject areas such as special education, mathematics, and science, and shortages in hard-to-staff schools in remote rural and urban school districts.[24] The rationale has been that teachers prepared through alternative routes would allegedly be better equipped and presumably do a better job of teaching, staying longer than the emergency-licensed teachers currently filling teaching vacancies. Hawley labels this rationale for alternative certification the "last resort" position: "It is argued when conventionally certified teachers cannot be found, it is better to have formal programs for recruiting, preparing, and supporting prospective teachers than it is to use emergency licensing procedures to fill teaching vacancies."[25]

With regard to the practical problem of filling vacant teaching positions, Feistritzer and Haar argue that alternative routes to teaching are more "efficient" than traditional programs because for various reasons, many individuals who are certified to teach after completing traditional college- and university-based programs do not teach (at least initially).[26] Most, if not all, teachers who enter the field through alternative routes do so because they intend to teach right away, and also, because many alternative routes are targeted to address specific shortages in particular locations.

Another reason why alternative routes to teaching have been approved by states has been to draw into teaching individuals who might not otherwise consider becoming teachers. For example, there has been a desire to use alternative certification to attract more people of color into the field of education so that the nation's teaching force will better reflect the diversity of society, and of pupils in the public schools.[27] There has also been a desire to draw more mature individuals with more varied life experiences into teaching—a population quite different from the typical college and university preservice teachers. It has been argued that the maturity and life experiences of teacher candidates are directly related to their potential to succeed in urban schools.[28] Alternative certification programs have been used in some cases to try and bring more men, mid-career changers, and retired military personnel into teaching—individuals, it was argued, who would not otherwise consider a career in teaching if the only option available to them was a traditional college or university program.[29]

Some advocates of alternative certification programs have expressed dissatisfaction with college and university teacher-education programs for allegedly not supplying teachers who are willing to teach in the schools that most need them, and/or for the perceived quality of teachers they have produced.[30] Others, such as Bliss, have argued that alternative certification can serve as a catalyst for the reform of college and university teacher education. Wisniewski argued that the development of alternative routes to teaching provides an opportunity for researchers to test the efficacy of different approaches to teacher education.[31]

Eubanks and Parish argued that traditional teacher-education programs have added to the inequitable access to fully certified teachers and to those teaching in their fields of expertise. They further believe that these programs contribute to the achievement gaps between pupils from different backgrounds by preparing teachers who do not want to teach in high-need schools—or, if they actually do end up teaching in these schools, they ultimately do not stay very long. Today, this inequitable distribution of teachers continues to negatively shape the education of poor children and children of color.[32]

Some critics of college and university teacher education who have expressed their dissatisfaction with these programs and the quality of their teacher candidates have fought for the deregulation of teacher education and the elimination of state certification requirements.[33] Under such plans, academically competent individuals with the desire to teach, but who are unwilling to enroll in a traditional college and university program, could enter teaching to supplant emergency-credentialed teachers. For these critics, college and university teacher education is seen as a barrier that keeps academically competent people out of teaching.

Those who advocate the increased influence of alternative routes believe that these programs would serve to raise the status of teaching as an occupation by bringing in many academically competent individuals who would not otherwise enter the field.[34] On the other hand, advocates of further professionalizing teaching and of strengthening college and university teacher education have argued that the spread of alternative routes will only serve to undermine the status of teaching by allowing people to enter the field with less preparation than is truly needed.[35]

Some proponents believe that alternative routes will expand the pool of available teachers, assuming that deregulation and a reduction in professional education requirements will bring academically competent individuals into teaching that have not previously chosen to enter the field, thereby raising the overall quality of the teaching pool. They also assume that these alternatively prepared teachers would be successful and choose to stay in teaching. The argument that is made today is very similar to the one made in the 1950s by those advocating the reduction of professional education requirements. For example, University of Illinois history professor Arthur Bestor asserted in a lecture at the University of Wyoming that by "dethroning these [professional education] requirements from their particularly privileged position,"[36] many academically talented individuals who do not choose to enroll in traditional college and university teacher-preparation programs would enter teaching.

> Young men and woman of genuine intellectual interest and capacity will be attracted in increasing numbers into the profession of teaching. They will not be repelled at the onset by being asked to lay aside their intellectual interests and fritter away their time in the courses of the pedagogues. Under a well ordered plan, the gateway to teaching will be the gateway to learning itself.[37]

In recent years, a new feature has emerged in the development of alternative routes into teaching: programs run by for-profit institutions and companies like the University of Phoenix, Kaplan, I-Teach Texas, and Laureate.[38] Consistent with efforts to privatize many aspects of life in advanced capitalist societies,[39] teacher education has become a business in the U.S.[40] This growth in proprietary programs has coincided with continuing cuts by many state governments in the level of support for public universities,[41] where the majority of teachers are still prepared.

Advocates of what has come to be called the "competitive model" for teacher certification[42] assert that subjecting teacher education and teacher certification to market forces will raise the quality of teacher preparation through the competition that results for the teacher-education market. For example, Hess has argued that through a competitive certification system driven by markets,

> . . . weaker teacher preparation programs would likely fall by the wayside. The fact that Schools of Education could no longer rely on a captive body of aspiring teachers would expose them to the cleansing winds of competition. Schools would have to contribute value by providing teacher training, services, or research that created demand and attracted support or face significant cutbacks.[43]

The federal government under the George W. Bush administration has actively encouraged the development of alternative certification programs—and a competitive certification system overall—by funding the establishment of a National Center for Alternative Certification.[44] The administration has supported these efforts by classifying teachers enrolled in alternative programs as "highly qualified" under the "No Child Left Behind" act, and by providing $40 million of start-up funding to the American Board for Certification of Teacher Excellence (ABCTE), which certifies teachers in seven states by written examination alone.

One clear example of the Bush administration's position in active support of a market-driven teacher certification system is the first annual Secretary of Education's Report on Teacher Quality. In this report, then secretary of education Rod Paige, a former school superintendent and dean of the College of Education at Texas Southern University, called for a streamlined teacher certification system in which attendance at college and university schools of education and unpaid student teaching would be optional: "Mandated education courses, unpaid student teaching, and the hoops and hurdles of the state certification bureaucracy discourage many potential teachers from entering the pipeline. The tragedy is that none of these hurdles leads to improved quality."[45]

CONTEXTS FOR ALTERNATIVE CERTIFICATION PROGRAMS

Within each state, the eligible providers create programs to implement the alternative routes to teacher certification. Upon successful completion of the state approved alternative route program and recommendations from the provider, the state certifies individuals to teach in the state. In 2006, nearly all of the 50,000 participants were teachers of record in schools across the country while they were being certified. Providers implemented 125 state alternative routes through an estimated 485 alternative route programs.[46]

Feistritzer traces the growth of alternative routes into teaching over the last two decades, from 1983—when eight states had authorized twelve programs—to 2006, when all fifty states and the District of Columbia had authorized 485 alternative programs. She notes that while in 1985 approximately 285 individuals entered teaching through alternative routes, nearly 59,000—or about one-third of newly hired teachers—did so in 2007. Although all states have now authorized these pathways to teaching, the growth of alternative routes to teaching has been concentrated in relatively few states in the East, West, and South, where there are large numbers of pupils in the public schools, and where the ability to find qualified teachers who are certified in the subjects that they are teaching is most challenging.[47] For example, they report that in 2005, the number of individuals certified through alternative routes in just three states—California, New Jersey, and Texas—accounted for nearly one-half of all teachers in the U.S. certified through alternative routes that year. In this same year, New Jersey reported that nearly 40 percent of new hires entered through alternative programs, while the percentage in Texas and California was about one-third.[48]

Alternative certification programs are extremely varied among and within states, ranging from those linked with master's degrees in colleges and universities, to the "Passport to Teaching" offered by the American Board for the Certification of Teacher Excellence, which enables individuals to be certified based on passing online subject-matter and professional knowledge tests.[49] Additionally, Feistritzer and Haar's national tabulation of data, as well as studies of individual alternative certification programs, have shown that there is much variation both within and between individual programs.[50] Alternative certification programs differ from one another in terms of:

- whom they try to attract (e.g., recent graduates of elite universities, paraprofessional educators, retired military, people from business and industry);
- their entry requirements;
- their courses and other program components;
- length of their program and how much of the candidate's preparation is completed prior to assuming responsibility for a classroom; and
- the nature and quality of mentoring and support that is provided once the trained teacher is in a classroom.

Some states require graduates of alternative routes to meet the same standards as those met by graduates of traditional college and university programs, while others allow less rigorous standards for alternative routes.[51]

In addition to colleges and universities, a variety of institutions have emerged to become the providers of alternative certification programs, including school districts, regional professional development centers, private companies, and community colleges. In addition, collaborations have been formed among different providers, such as between colleges and universities and school districts. Some alternative programs can legitimately be called "fast-track" programs because the length of time from enrollment to certification is shorter than typical college and university programs, but other alternative programs are as long as typical college and university postbaccalaureate programs. Some programs offer a curriculum very similar to that which exists in typical college and university programs, and others do not. It is very difficult to draw any conclusions about the nature of alternative certification programs as a whole. It should be noted that two programs frequently referred to as alternative certification programs—"Teach For America" (TFA) and "Troops to Teachers"—are, in reality, recruitment programs rather than certification programs. For example, TFA participants must complete other traditional and/or alternative programs beyond the common summer institute in order to become certified to teach.

CONCLUSION

Several conclusions can be reached from this brief analysis of alternative teacher certification programs in the U.S. The first is that pathways into teaching other than traditional college and university programs have been in existence throughout the history of American teacher education. The rapid development of alternative routes to teaching since the mid-1980s represents a reemergence of diversity in teacher-education pathways rather than a new phenomenon.

Second, the category of alternative certification programs is so broad that one cannot generalize individual virtues and shortcomings. In order to understand the nature and quality of a teacher-education program, one needs to have more information about its substance. Furthermore, in order to distinguish between illusory and genuine preparation, one needs to know the realities of each program, not merely the advertised characteristics. For example, in some cases teachers have said that they did not meet with their mentors in programs that were described in the literature as having a "mentoring component."[52]

Third, Wilson and Tamir rightly warn us with regard to how challengers to dominant forms of teacher education in the U.S. are perceived; it is an oversimplification to conclude that all proponents of alternatives to dominant practices hold the same political and ideological motivations.[53] They argue that essentializing the critics obscures the complexity of the issues. We can conclude from our brief analysis of the issue of alternative teacher certification that advocates of alternative routes to teaching, including "early-entry" programs, are supported by individuals and groups that represent a range of different political and ideological perspectives on schooling, teachers, and teacher education.[54]

Some advocates of alternative certification are indeed harsh critics of the value of teacher education in schools of education, and their advocacy of alternative routes represents a repudiation of traditional programs. We have seen, however, that there are other alternative certification advocates who are motivated by such things as a belief in the value of competition and markets, or by a desire to narrow the achievement gaps in public schools. These advocates are not necessarily seeking to eliminate the role of education schools in American teacher preparation. In fact, as Fenstermacher has pointed out, some advocates of traditional college and university preparation believe that "reputable forms" of alternative certification may have a positive impact on traditional forms of teacher education by encouraging experimentation and innovation.[55] Clearly, the debate over alternative and traditional forms of teacher education is much more complex than is often portrayed by both its opponents and proponents, and in the media.

Also, given the large number of teachers that we need to prepare for our public schools, there will likely continue to be a need for multiple pathways into teaching that address the different circumstances of individuals who desire to teach. Alternative teacher certification programs situated outside of colleges and universities have been perceived by some as a threat to the existence of "college-recommending" teacher education, in part because of the active support of alternative programs by the current administration in Washington—while support for public universities, teacher-education research, and teacher-education programs continues to decline.[56] This positioning of "college-recommending" programs *against* "early-entry programs" will not help us address the numerous problems that exist in our public schools today.

In our view, research on alternative pathways into teaching should focus on identifying the program features that are most effective for preparing particular kinds of individuals to teach in specific kinds of schools. Recent research has identified a number of program characteristics that warrant further study.[57] The task for policymakers should be to make sure that these features are present in *all* teacher-education programs, both traditional and alternative. If we continue to seek evidence that any one model of teacher education is superior to others and to ignore the wide range of quality that exists within all models, we will continue to be disappointed in the results.

Finally, in thinking about the issue of pathways into teaching, we must not lose sight of the need to invest in public colleges and universities so that they are able to provide high-quality teacher education. The existence—and even the growth—of alternative routes into teaching do not necessarily mean that we should continue the national trend of reducing the percentage of states' contributions to college and university budgets. This constant decline of resources has negatively affected the ability of colleges and universities to meet the new accountability demands and maintain a high quality of teacher preparation.[58] It is possible to simultaneously invest in both traditional and alternative forms of teacher certification. We also should not neglect the need to improve salaries and working conditions for teachers, and to fully fund public schools at a level that enables educators to do the job we expect of them.[59] The issue of identifying productive pathways into teaching is an important one, but it cannot be isolated from a societal commitment to strengthening our public schools and to providing all citizens with the necessities within and beyond schooling to lead their lives with dignity.

CHAPTER 2

Who Goes into Early-Entry Programs?

Karen Hammerness and Michelle Reininger

The demographics of teachers—who they *are* and who people think they *should be*—rests at the center of many of the debates about early-entry certification. In response to concerns that teachers' qualifications have been diminishing, some educators argue that early-entry certification programs can recruit more academically successful people into the profession. Others, concerned about the lack of diversity in the teaching population, have argued that early-entry certification programs might attract teachers with more varied ethnic and racial backgrounds.[1] Still others, who point to the need for teachers with greater content-area knowledge, have also argued that these programs can attract into teaching mid-career professionals who have expertise in high-need subject areas, such as science and mathematics.[2]

In short, many hopes and expectations surround the kind of teachers early-entry certification could potentially attract. However, we need to know much more about the nature of the demographics of early-entry certification teachers. To what extent do they fit the expectations, hopes, and ideas of those who have argued that such a pathway will attract a new kind of candidate for teaching? Are these early-entry-certified teachers more racially diverse, professionally experienced, and academically strong? Or do they, instead, fulfill the concerns of those worried about the lack of qualification and experience of those entering through early-entry pathways? While early-entry certification is not a new phenomenon, the proliferation of these programs has occurred at a surprising rate in the past ten years (see chapter 1 of this volume, "The Development of Alternative Certification Policies and Programs in the United States").[3] Not surprisingly, research on who enters these programs is still relatively new and, given the rapid growth of early-entry programs, studies conducted even a few years ago can seem out-of-date.

In this chapter, we review research on who uses early-entry certification pathways for becoming a teacher. We focus on the most current research in this area, but we also include research from the recent past. In addition, while much of the research we share has been conducted nationally, we also provide data from our own work studying teacher-preparation pathways in New York City.[4] A focus upon a particular setting for early-entry programs—and the candidates in specific programs—can help illuminate some of the questions and challenges surrounding the qualifications of teachers in these programs. Our sample includes twenty-six traditional programs and the two largest early-entry programs supplying teachers to New York City. In this way we provide a lens into the demographics of teachers for one particular urban school environment, to help shed light upon some of the ways in which a particular context can contribute to understanding variations and similarities across state and national levels. In addition, we are able to compare survey responses from the participants in the two early-entry programs as well as compare responses across traditional and early-entry programs.

Current research on teacher-preparation programs suggests that preparation programs are not monolithic, and comparing within and across all programs—early-entry and traditional—is essential in order to get a comprehensive picture of the differences between programs and pathways. Much of the expansion in early-entry certification in the past ten years has been seen in specialized programs, designed to attract a very specific population to teaching or to meet the staffing needs of a particular state, district, or even school.

The chapter is organized around four questions:

- What are the demographics of early-entry candidates?
- What do they bring to teaching?
- What factors led them to select an early-entry route?; and
- Where are they choosing to teach?

DEMOGRAPHICS OF EARLY-ENTRY CANDIDATES

Proponents of early-entry certification routes argue that creating these new pathways is an important way to diversify the demographics of the teacher workforce. These new entry routes may appeal to individuals who do not have a "typical" teacher profile. Nationally, the teacher labor force is made up of predominantly white females: Three out of four elementary and secondary school teachers are women, and eight out of ten are white.[5] While no national study of all early-entry certification routes exists, many empirical studies provide insight into the types of candidates some early-entry programs are attracting.

Gender

Women have made up the overwhelming majority of the teacher workforce over the past half century. One hope of early-entry routes is that they may attract more men into the profession. Recent research indicates that assignment to a same-gender teacher significantly improves the achievement of boys and girls.[6] Some recent empirical studies confirm that, in fact, early-entry programs are attracting more men into teaching. For instance, Feistritzer conducted a survey of 2,647 teachers entering teaching through early-entry routes in Florida and Texas, as well as a sample of candidates in the Troops to Teachers program (TTT), the Milwaukee Teacher Education Center program (MTEC), and the New York City Teaching Fellows (NYCTF) program.[7] In her survey, Feistritzer found that 37 percent of the early-entry candidate population was male, well above the national average of 25 percent. It is possible that the low overall survey response rate and the inclusion of the TTT program in her sample, however, affect the averages she reports.[8]

Research on individuals preparing for teaching in the New York City area by pathway and by program also found more men entering through early-entry routes. Of the participants in the two early-entry programs surveyed in NYC, Teach For America (TFA) and New York City Teaching Fellows (NYCTF), men made up 30 and 31 percent of the candidates, respectively, as compared to 22 percent in the traditional graduate programs, and only 7 percent in the traditional undergraduate programs.[9]

On the other hand, not all data from recent empirical studies find more men entering through early-entry routes. Humphrey and Wechsler[10] studied a sample of participants in seven early-entry certification programs and found that, on average, these programs attract the same proportion of males and females as currently exist in the national labor market: "about three-quarters of participants are women, a number consistent with the national average for all teachers."[11] However, they also call attention to the substantial variation by program. TFA, for instance, tends to attract more male participants, and Humphrey and Wechsler note that men account for up to 43 percent of the participants in the New Jersey Provisional Teacher Program. On the other hand, they find that only 34 percent of those in the Texas Region XIII program are male.

Data collected almost fifteen years ago suggests a similar finding. In her analysis of the 1993–94 Schools and Staffing Survey (SASS), Shen also finds little difference in gender between traditionally and early-entry-certified teachers. According to Shen, 24 percent of traditionally certified teachers were male, while men made up 26 percent of the early-entry-certified teachers.[12]

In sum, the research does not consistently suggest that there are more male teachers in early-entry pathways. While some recent evidence suggests that there are more men, other research calls attention to significant variation across programs. However, because there are still few studies that examine the gender of entrants across many different pathways, as well as within early-entry programs, it is difficult to draw firm conclusions as to whether early-entry programs are attracting more men into teaching.

Race and Ethnicity

The racial and ethnic composition of the teacher workforce is quite different than that of the student population. While only 17 percent of teachers are nonwhite, over 40 percent of elementary and secondary students are nonwhite.[13] This lack of minority teachers may have important consequences for minority student learning. Using data from the Tennessee STAR class-size experiment, Thomas Dee finds that random assignment to a racially similar teacher improved the test scores of both black and white students.[14] Educators interested in diversifying the workforce to help address the lack of minority teachers have argued that early-entry routes may appeal in particular to teachers of color who may wish to enter the classroom more rapidly, as well as earn a salary during preparation.

Some research does suggest that early-entry programs do attract a greater proportion of teachers of color. For instance, in New York City, while the majority of all participants in teacher-preparation programs in 2003–04 were white, the early-entry pathways did have higher percentages of teachers of color. In both TFA and the NYCTF, slightly over half of the candidates were white (58 percent and 56 percent, respectively), while 67 and 63 percent (respectively) of traditional undergraduate and graduate certification candidates were white. In the NYCTF program, 15 percent of participants were African American, and 12 percent were Hispanic. And, in TFA, 8 percent were African American, 10 percent Hispanic, and 25 percent "other."[15] Feistritzer also found in her sample that 32 percent of early-entry certification candidates were nonwhite, and even more (37%) of the candidates in her sample of Troops to Teachers were teachers of color.[16] In her TTT sample, she found that almost one-quarter of the teachers were black and 9 percent were Hispanic.

Similarly, Humphrey and Wechsler found that for all seven early-entry programs they studied, minority teachers made up 40 percent of participants.[17] However, Humphrey and Wechsler also call attention again to variations that exist across the programs, suggesting that the differences may reflect the local teacher labor market. For example,

> . . . about 36 percent of the Texas Region XIII participants are African American or Hispanic. Although higher than the national average, that percentage is just slightly more than the 29 percent of teachers in Austin (the largest district served by the Region XIII program) who are African American or Hispanic.[18]

They also mention that one program, Milwaukee's Metropolitan Multicultural Teacher Education Program (MMTEP), stood out, with 80 percent of participants who are people of color. They explain that not only was this the highest percentage of the seven programs they studied, but it was also substantially higher than the proportion of teachers of color in the Milwaukee Public Schools.

This may be explained, they say, by the fact that one of the program's primary goals was to recruit and prepare teachers of color. The existing evidence supports the claim that early-entry certification may increase the aggregate percentage of racial minorities who enter the teacher workforce, and programs aimed specifically at minority recruitment, like the MMTEP, can be very successful. Even in the cases where the composition of the local labor market has an above-average percentage of minority teachers, the profile of those candidates coming from the early-entry pathways mirrors, if not exceeds, the local conditions. However, as with gender, the evidence also suggests variation by program and labor market, in that some programs in some state contexts stood out as having many more candidates of color than others.

Age

Another belief about early-entry routes is that they may attract older individuals into teaching, hence bringing a level of maturity, sense of responsibility, and commitment that younger individuals may not yet have.[19] Data from the 1999–2000 and the 2003–04 SASS indicates that the average age of beginning teachers in the U.S. is twenty-nine years old.[20] Given that more and more young adults expect to have more than one career in their lifetime, some have argued that older adults who may now be seeking a second career represent a promising population from which to recruit new teachers. [21]

Some reports on early-entry certification candidates do suggest that early-entry candidates are indeed slightly older than the average beginning teacher. Feistritzer found that of the early-entry program participants she surveyed, 72 percent were age thirty or older, 47 percent were forty and older, and 20 percent were older than fifty.[22] However, Feistritzer does not provide an analysis of the age breakdown by program, and other studies suggest that there may be significant variation in age across different early-entry certification programs.[23]

Humphrey and Wechsler found that the participants in the seven early-entry certification programs they studied were, on average, approximately thirty-two years of age.[24] However, they also noted that participants' ages varied greatly across programs. Participants in TFA, for example, were substantially younger than the national average, while participants in other programs, such as North Carolina's NCTEACH and MMTEP, were older. They attribute the variation in age, in part, to program recruiting practices: "TFA targets recent college graduates from selective universities, whereas MMTEP focuses on applicants with classroom experience and admits only those who have at least one year of experience as a teacher's assistant."[25]

In New York City, the results confirm such variation among early-entry certification programs. However, the results also suggest, surprisingly, that early-entry pathways do *not* necessarily attract candidates older than those in traditional teaching programs. For instance, in an analysis of our survey of 2,048 participants from traditional programs and from Teach For America and the New York City Teaching Fellows during the 2003–04 academic year, we found that participants in Teach For America were, in fact, the youngest of all the participants, averaging twenty-two years. Surprisingly, TFA candidates were even younger than students in the traditional *undergraduate* programs, whose average age was twenty-three. The New York City Teaching Fellows were older than TFA candidates, averaging twenty-eight years of age. However, also unexpectedly, we found that the oldest students in our sample were not those in early-entry pathways, but rather the students in traditional graduate programs, whose average age was thirty.

Research from the past seems consistent with some of the current findings that suggest early-entry pathways may not attract an older population. In her analysis of the 1993–94 SASS survey, Shen found a larger number of younger teachers in the early-entry-certified sample, while there were more teachers over age fifty in the traditionally certified sample.[26] Shen concludes, in fact, that early-entry certification programs were unsuccessful in meeting their goal of bringing older teachers into the workforce.

In sum, the results do not consistently suggest that participants in early-entry certification programs are older. Rather, the age of candidates seems to vary by program, and actually, some results across the last fifteen years suggest that traditional programs, not early-entry programs, may attract older participants. This may, however, be due to the fact that a number of alternative programs—particularly the well-known or national ones, such as TFA—specifically target recent college graduates. So it may not be that older individuals prefer traditional programs, but, rather, that many of the alternative programs are not designed to recruit them.

At the same time, it is important to note that whether older candidates represent a preferable population from which to recruit remains an empirical question. While some argue that older candidates may bring maturity, responsibility, and commitment to the field, others have noted that older candidates could just as well be less reliable and responsible, having left prior careers for new ones. Furthermore, whether older individuals bring an increased level of experience, expertise, and content knowledge also remains underexplored.

BUNDLES OF CHARACTERISTICS OR CATEGORIES

While it is useful to examine specific aspects of early-entry candidates, such as age or gender or race, it is also possible that there are other ways of characterizing these participants that move beyond discrete descriptive data. Some research has focused upon developing "profiles" of early-entry candidates that will shed light upon sets of features that seem to characterize groups of participants, in order to better understand the motivations, perceptions of teaching, and plans for the future that these groups might bring to teaching.[27]

For instance, Crow, Levine, and Nager examined patterns among teachers' perceptions of teaching, beliefs about their past work, and the degree to which the candidates still identified with that prior work.[28] They found that three patterns seemed to characterize their participants. They named the first group *homecomers*, arguing that for them, the term "career changer" seemed a bit inaccurate, as they had not necessarily pursued a true "career" prior to becoming a teacher. However, these teachers felt as if they had always dreamed of being a teacher, and for them, teaching represented a kind of psychological homecoming. The second group, which they call *the converted*, consisted of participants who did not seriously consider teaching "until some pivotal event or confluence of factors caused them to reconsider professional plans." They labeled the last group *the unconverted*, describing them as having achieved high status (like the converted) in other occupations, but who did not feel, after having tried teaching, that it was the right occupation for them; this group did not plan to remain in teaching. This study was conducted with a small sample of individuals in one teacher-education program designed for mid-career entrants, and understanding more about the degree to which different early-entry candidates may fall into these categories would be useful for recruitment and preparation.

ATTITUDES ABOUT THE PROFESSION
AND THE WORK OF TEACHING

Chin and Young characterized early-entry teachers by their perspective on teaching and professional careers.[29] They described the teachers they studied not by specific demographic features, but rather by the broader categories that seemed to capture their approaches to work and to teaching. They found that their sample of early-entry teachers fell into six groups, which they termed: career changers, socially committed, compatible life-stylists, working-class activists, romantic idealists, and career explorers. To some degree, the composition of these groups differed by race, gender, and ethnicity, suggesting that these kinds of groupings could be useful in understanding these types of teacher candidates, as well as understanding their motivations and beliefs about teaching. This knowledge could be particularly valuable in recruiting a more-diverse pool of teachers.

Similarly, Johnson and her colleagues draw upon data from interviews and surveys with fifty new teachers (both mid-career and first-career entrants) who entered teaching through early-entry and traditional certification pathways.[30] They identify two orientations toward the profession, expressed by teachers in both pathways. One group, whom they termed *explorers*, was not sure about whether or not they would stay in teaching (although they might, given good conditions and appropriate rewards). The second, whom they termed *contributors*, saw teaching as one, but not the only, way to make a contribution to society. The researchers emphasize that these groups of teachers did not consider teaching a trivial pursuit and intended to teach with passion, commitment, and serious effort—but planned to do so only for a short time. Understanding more about which populations of teachers take these approaches to the teaching profession could be particularly useful in designing targeted recruitment or induction programs.

MID-CAREER ENTRANTS

Another, broader category that often comes up in discussions of early-entry certification is that of "mid-career entrant" or "career changer." Some educators and policymakers have argued that there is a population of professionals eager to teach but who may be dissuaded from actually becoming a teacher by the burdensome requirements of traditional teacher education; and that early-entry programs represent an attractive alternative that would appeal to such candidates.[31] These candidates would use early-entry certification programs to switch from a professional career such as law or engineering into teaching, bringing with them the strong content-area knowledge accumulated in their previous careers.[32] Yet it is important to know whether in fact substantial numbers of these candidates exist and whether they should remain a central focus of policy efforts to recruit them.

Some researchers have argued that there is a fair amount of evidence that early-entry programs *do* bring more mid-career entrants into teaching. In the recent past, Shen concluded that there were more candidates entering as mid-career entrants in early-entry programs than in traditional programs.[33] Others who studied this phenomenon seem to agree: Ruenzel, who looked at statewide data in California, and Chin, Young, and Floyd, who studied an early-entry program in California, found entrants in the program to have an average age of thirty-five.[34] Feistritzer's data also showed that 72 percent of entrants were over thirty.[35] Johnson argues that there are a growing number of older or mid-career entrants choosing teaching as a profession, and that they should be considered in policy discussions.[36]

However, while these researchers do provide evidence of a growing number of older entrants, they do not have data on the prior occupations of these entrants; therefore, we cannot assume these candidates come from professional careers. Furthermore, they can only infer that these mid-career entrants come through early-entry routes, as they do not have data providing evidence of the type of preparation these teachers selected.[37] Finally, it is important to note that this data infers entrants are "career changers" based upon their age of entry, and a high age may, in fact, simply indicate a longer undergraduate career, or that candidates have pursued different positions or careers, or an absence from paid work in the labor market. In that case, it may not be appropriate to term these candidates "career changers," and may be more useful to categorize them in some other way that might better capture their previous work history.

Indeed, a recent review of the literature on older entrants into teaching raises questions about the notion of the "mid-career" or "second-career" teacher, and in particular, points to assumptions regarding age and work experience in much research on older entrants. Hammerness found that it is not entirely clear how many *true* mid-career entrants exist, nor whether early-entry programs adequately recruit such candidates.[38] While this review found a number of studies that suggested older candidates are entering teaching through alternative routes, little evidence exists to suggest that large numbers of these candidates are in fact professionals seeking a true "second career." Rather, the candidates seemed to fall into three categories. The first consisted of fairly recent graduates, some even still in their mid-twenties, who have not yet settled on a career but did not enter teaching right out of college/university.

The second consisted of candidates in their thirties and forties. Within this group, some are well-trained men and women who have pursued a prior career, such as law, medicine, or engineering, and have chosen to pursue teaching as a second career. However, others have pursued more than one occupation before settling upon teaching. Still others may have had an administrative or clerical position, but not a professional position for which prior training or graduate preparation was required. For some of the candidates in this group, teaching may in fact represent an increase in salary and professional status as opposed to a step down.

The third group represents those candidates in their fifties or sixties who may be at the end of a career, and are seeking a new position in retirement. However, research has not yet been able to determine with certainty how many of these different candidates exist, which might be most desirable in teaching, nor their motivations and plans for teaching. The notion of the mid-career candidate needs far greater elaboration and understanding.

Indeed, Humphrey and Wechsler note that in their sample of early-entry candidates, even though there were many mid-career changers in their sample,

> relatively few participants switched from careers in mathematics and science to teaching (about 5 percent). Only 2 percent came from the legal profession, and 6 percent from a financial or accounting career. In contrast, about 42 percent of participants were either in education or were full-time students immediately before entering their early entry certification program.

And, although they note that many advocates of mid-career entrants argue that there are those willing to take pay cuts to become teachers, they found few in their sample who actually took such cuts, reporting that "59 percent of participants in fact received a pay raise by becoming teachers."[39]

In our New York sample, we, too, found that the early-entry pathways did not necessarily attract a sample of teachers who had substantial professional experience outside of education. In fact, the mean experience in a professional position outside of education was almost exactly the same for both traditional graduate participants and for the Teaching Fellows, with the traditional graduates actually reporting slightly more experience.

In sum, examining early-entry candidates' profiles and backgrounds may be a particularly important development in research on early-entry pathways. Understanding the kinds of motivations, beliefs about teaching, and plans for the future could be especially useful in designing appropriate incentives, preparation, and supports that could attract different populations of potential teachers. However, much more research needs to be conducted in this area—particularly in order to move beyond designations such as "mid-career entrant" that still do not fully capture the range of backgrounds, work experiences, and motivations of different groups of candidates for teaching.

WHAT QUALIFICATIONS DO EARLY ENTRANTS BRING TO TEACHING?

Another key policy question concerns the kind of qualifications and previous experiences early-entry teachers bring to teaching. Some have argued that early-entry candidates bring subject-area expertise and strong content knowledge, while others suggest that this may not be the case. In this section, we shed light upon what is known about the kinds of qualifications—the academic backgrounds, the subject-area expertise, previous work experiences and experiences with children, and additional knowledge of languages—that these individuals may bring to teaching, and how they may differ from those of teachers who come to teaching through more traditional pathways.

Academic Background

Advocates of early-entry certification have frequently argued that these pathways and programs could attract an academically better-prepared population, who might otherwise be discouraged by the lower status of education courses and schools and the perception of such programs as less academically engaging.[40] Such arguments also emphasize the notion that those who have previously completed bachelor's degrees in fields other than education may not be willing to put time or effort into additional training, and that early-entry pathways may be of particular appeal to those potential teachers. A number of common measures are used to capture the academic effectiveness of teachers, including: highest level of education, selectivity of undergraduate institution, and content knowledge as measured by college subject-area majors. However, empirical research demonstrates that only some of these characteristics have been linked to effective teaching. In a review of the literature, Loeb and Reininger highlight a number of studies that have found student achievement improves more in classes in which the teachers have higher test scores or have attended selective undergraduate institutions.[41] Other studies have found that greater content knowledge for high school teachers also improves student outcomes. Interestingly, even though nearly half of all teachers have earned master's degrees, there is no evidence that having a master's degree improves a teacher's ability in the classroom.[42]

In Humphrey and Wechsler's study of seven early-entry certification programs, they did find that, overall, early-entry-route teachers are more likely to have graduated from competitive institutions of higher education than from noncompetitive ones.[43] However, they also found substantial variation in the selectivity of the colleges attended by the program participants. For instance, in their sample, the percentage of early-entry certification participants attending a competitive college ranged from 79 percent (TFA participants) to 6 percent (MMTEP participants). Given that Teach For America directly targets recruitment efforts at graduates from the most competitive colleges across the country, this is not surprising, yet it still calls attention to the wide range of academic backgrounds early-entry candidates are likely to have.

Feistritzer looked at two measures of academic achievement of the early-entry-certified participants in her sample: highest degree earned and area of college major.[44] She found that the percentage of early-entry-certified teachers with a bachelor's degree in a field other than education was quite high, 57 percent, compared with those with a bachelor's degree in education, only 3 percent. She also reports that those with a master's degree made up 37 percent of the sample (of which 19 percent had a master's in education and 18 percent in fields outside of education). While she does not provide data by program, in another study she reports that of the Troops to Teachers sample, 62 percent held a master's degree or higher. She found that, of the 2,554 respondents to the question, 23 have a law degree, 8 a medical degree, 27 a doctorate in a field other than education, 5 a doctorate in education, and 86 hold a bachelor's degree in education as their highest academic degree.[45]

Surveys of teacher candidates in New York City reveal that early-entry-certified teachers have had more math preparation in high school than traditionally certified candidates, but also reveal substantial variation between early-entry programs. Fifty-eight percent of TFA and 42 percent of Teaching Fellows participants had taken calculus in high school, while only 31 and 25 percent of traditionally certified graduate students and undergraduate students respectively had taken calculus in high school. However, limiting the sample to those teachers who are specifically preparing to be mathematics teachers, the two early-entry programs revealed a substantial range when it came to those who had taken calculus in high school: over 90 percent of TFA participants as compared to only 54 percent of Teaching Fellows participants. And, of traditionally certified teachers in our sample who were preparing to teach math, 43 percent of undergraduates and 42 percent of graduates had taken calculus.

Another indicator of educational background is parents' highest degree. In the New York City sample of early-entry and traditionally certified, we found more differences between programs than within pathways. For example, an equal percentage of participants (about 10 percent in each program) in the New York City Teaching Fellows program, traditional undergraduates, and traditional graduates reported the highest level of parent education was a high school degree. However, TFA participants stood out as outliers in this respect: Only 2 percent of TFA participants reported having parents with high school education as their highest degree.

It does appear that some early-entry pathways are attracting a more highly academically credentialed pool of teachers, but overall the existing research suggests that the bulk of the variation in a teacher's academic background exists between programs, and is not completely differentiated along pathway distinctions. Somewhat surprisingly, given the emphasis upon the subject-area expertise possessed by early-entry candidates—and older entrants in particular—there are no studies of early-entry mid-career candidates' content knowledge or subject backgrounds.[46]

Previous Work Experience and Work with Children

Of the many reasons for policymakers and educators' interest in attracting early-entry candidates into teaching, the perception that these candidates may have important skills and work experiences remains one of the most important. For instance, Johnson et al., who studied a sample of mid-career and first-career teachers in Massachusetts, found that their sample of twenty-four mid-career teachers—many of whom entered through early-entry programs—did have substantial work experiences.[47] They note that their sample

> brought with them a familiarity with large and small organizations, for-profit and non-profit enterprises, entrepreneurial and bureaucratic settings. Some had worked for multiple supervisors, whereas others had been supervisors themselves. They

worked freelance or led teams. Some experienced well-defined, progressive on the job training, and some devised training for other employees.

Feistritzer also found evidence that candidates are changing from professional careers to become teachers:

Nearly half (47%) of the people entering teaching through alternative routes were working in a noneducation job the year before they began an alternative route to a teacher certfication program. Forty percent were working in a professional occupation outside the field of education.[48]

On the other hand, other recent research has found few early-entry candidates with degrees in law or business, and with professional experience.[49] Furthermore, several studies found that a number of early-entry candidates received a pay raise when moving into teaching.[50] This finding underscores the fact that the assumption that all early-entry candidates come from high-paying, high-status professional experiences may be mistaken—given that some candidates, in fact, had prior positions that paid less than a teaching salary. Of course, it is worth noting that at least some of these participants in the Humphrey and Wechsler study had been teachers' aides and support staff in schools and were entering from paraprofessional programs. Past research confirms that early-entry candidates vary in terms of the nature of their prior work, some candidates coming from clerical or support positions as opposed to professional positions.[51]

Then again, Feistritzer's research suggests that more early-entry candidates had classroom experience.[52] While she found that about 40 percent were in what she referred to as a "professional" occupation, 17 percent had been in a teaching-related job (such as a substitute teacher, or preschool teacher). Indeed, critics of poor-quality early-entry routes to teaching often point to candidates' lack of prior classroom experience and background in child development as shortcomings that result in underprepared teachers. However, Johnson and colleagues contend that older entrants potentially have more firsthand understanding of children's development due to the experience of having had their own children.[53]

Despite the potential importance candidates' experience in schools and with children could have for teaching, only a few studies exist that directly examine the level of experience early-entry candidates have had in schools and with children. Of those, Humphrey and Wechsler found that many of their early-entry certification teachers had experience in classrooms before beginning the certification programs.[54] More than one-third of the participants in three of the programs they studied had worked as classroom teachers, substitutes, or teacher's aides at some time in their careers. They also add that, in five of the seven programs, more than 60 percent of their participants report some previous classroom experience. Again, the experience varied by program, yet across all programs, participants seemed to have had more experiences with children and in classrooms than expected. They report:

New Jersey's Provisional Teacher Program attracted the largest number of participants with prior teaching experience. Half of the participants had an average of 39 months of teaching experience. For some, the duration of their prior experience may be related to the timing of their participation in the program. Specifically, some participants had started teaching, but could not attend program classes because of paperwork delays at the New Jersey State Department of Education. Further, while only 14 percent of New York City Teaching Fellows had prior experience as a classroom teacher, those participants had an average of 40 months of teaching experience.[55]

When the New York City Pathways study researchers gathered information from candidates about their previous work experiences, they surveyed both early-entry candidates and traditional candidates, allowing for a comparison between the two groups. In terms of previous teaching experience, the results show that those in traditional programs were more likely to have previous teaching experience (such as a full-time teacher, preschool teacher, or a substitute teacher) than the early-entry candidates. However, those within the early-entry programs did indicate they had more experience working with low-income children in urban settings prior to beginning their certification program than those in the traditional programs. The participants in the traditional graduate and Teaching Fellows programs had, on average, more experience working in professional positions both within and outside of the field of education than the younger undergraduate and TFA candidates, which may likely be a result of their older age.

In contradiction to many critics who worry that early-entry certification teachers are inexperienced and untrained with regard to children and schools, several of these large studies do suggest that these teachers bring some previous classroom experience with children. However, few of the studies looked specifically at the nature of the student populations with which the candidates worked. Given a recent study by Public Agenda which found that 64 percent of new teachers from early-entry pathways (as compared to 41 percent of traditionally trained new entrants) felt they were placed in schools with children who were described as "the hardest to reach," knowing whether the candidates have any past experience with such children could be extremely useful.[56]

In sum, it seems possible that early entrants may have more experience in schools and with children than has been assumed. On the other hand, more research needs to be pursued in order to understand the nature of the experiences these entrants have had in education, and with particular populations of students, as well as what role their own experiences (if any) as parents may play.

Knowledge of Languages

Accompanying the growing racial and ethnic diversity of the student population is the rapid expansion of the number of students who are classified as English-language learners (ELLs). Teachers who are fluent in languages other than English may have the advantage of being able to talk with students and their families in the native language of the family as well as acting as a resource for their schools. By bringing in teachers with more language diversity, early-entry routes may be helping to fill an unmet need of many students, families, and schools.

Natriello and Zumwalt found that early-entry certification candidates in New Jersey were more likely to speak a language other than English.[57] Similarly, more recent survey results from teacher candidates in NYC suggest that early-entry pathways are increasing the language diversity of teachers. Preservice teacher candidates were asked if they spoke another language besides English fluently, and 41 percent of those in TFA and 35 percent of NYC Teaching Fellows indicated they did. Of the candidates in traditional certification programs, 32 percent of undergraduates and only one-quarter of candidates in the graduate programs indicated they spoke another language fluently. While these studies suggest that early-entry pathways could be bringing in individuals with more language and racial diversity, more work in this area needs to be pursued.

WHAT FACTORS LED CANDIDATES TO CONSIDER AN EARLY-ENTRY ROUTE?

Proponents claim key factors that attract candidates into early-entry programs include shortened preparation time, quick entry into the classroom, and convenience of the program. But the question remains as to whether candidates themselves report those factors as being important. Or are other factors, including the ability to earn an income while attending school, at play? In this section, we address these questions as well as the key issue: whether these entrants might have used a more traditional pathway if these early-entry programs did not exist.

When asked about the factors that were most important in selecting an early-entry certification program, data from multiple studies suggest that individuals emphasize the importance of financial cost, length of time, and convenience.[58] For example, in a report specifically focused upon early-entry certification programs and participants in four states (Connecticut, Massachusetts, California, and Louisiana), Johnson and her colleagues found that a similar series of characteristics appealed to the participants. Data interviews of eighty participants in these programs suggested that they appreciated the fact that the programs offered "faster, less expensive, more practical, and more convenient training, sometimes with the promise of job placement."[59]

Feistritzer reports similar findings.[60] She finds that variables respondents rated as *very important* in choosing an alternate route to teacher certification included: receiving a teacher's salary and benefits (76%); being able to teach while getting certified (73%); out-of-pocket costs (57%); and length of program (57%). Interestingly, the variables that ranked highest in the *not at all important* category in Feistritzer's survey were: being able to get a master's degree (26%); guidance from college faculty (21%); and being able to go through the program in a cohort (17%).

Our results from NYC echo these sentiments as well. Candidates in early-entry certification pathways place high importance on ease of transition into teaching, low cost of the program, and ability to sustain a steady income; however, a more detailed look at the responses reveals interesting variation between pathways. On a survey in which traditional and early-entry respondents were asked to indicate the top three reasons, from a list of twenty-four, that were most important for the selection of their teacher-education program, significant differences were found to exist between those in the TFA program and the NYC Teaching Fellows programs. The top reasons reported by those in the NYCTF program include ease of transition from a non-teaching career, ability to sustain a steady income, and low tuition, while the top reasons given by TFA respondents include program's mission, program reputation, and intellectual challenge. Comparing across early-entry and traditional pathways shows that those in the traditional programs rank items similar to those in the Teaching Fellows program as the most important for their program choice, including low tuition, ease of transition from a non-teaching career, and flexibility of classes. Clearly, however, the population of candidates who select a program such as Teach For America may find different factors important—and the importance of program aims and goals, reputation, and intellectual challenge is a set of factors not often recognized in the design of early-entry programs.

A few studies have looked at the role of these particular factors in alternative teachers' decisionmaking in more depth. For instance, in light of policymakers' attempts to address candidates' potential concerns about salary loss or other financial issues, some studies have examined the role that monetary incentives—such as signing bonuses, grants, and stipends—play in candidates' decisionmaking. Two studies have examined the impact of signing bonuses offered by the Massachusetts Initiative for New Teachers (MINT) program, which included an unprecedented $20,000 signing bonus.[61] In their study of thirteen individuals entering teaching through this program, Johnson and Liu found that the chance to avoid the "opportunity costs" of loss of income coupled with the potential out-of-pocket costs for tuition, was much more important to the participants than the signing bonus.[62] While this may seem surprising, Johnson and Liu argue that in fact, the opportunity costs could have greatly exceeded the $20,000 amount they received as a bonus. As they contend, "the bonus money itself was a relatively weak incentive. A much more powerful extrinsic incentive, according to virtually all participants, was the program's accelerated route to certification."[63] Indeed, they found that while the bonuses helped make some teachers' transitions to teaching easier, ultimately, they played "virtually no role" in teachers' decisions about whether or not to remain in the profession. Rather, the single most important influence was the "intrinsic rewards of teaching and the respondents' success in realizing them."[64] Relatedly, a recent survey conducted by Public Agenda with new teachers from three alternative routes (Teach For America, the New Teachers Project, and Troops to Teachers) suggested that the majority (71%) of new teachers from alternative routes surveyed "say they would rather work in a school where 'administrators gave strong backing and support' compared with a school where they could earn more."[65]

Finally, one key critique of early-entry route programs is that they are diverting individuals who would otherwise obtain more substantial and thorough preparation through traditional pathways. Few large studies have attempted to determine whether this is in fact the case or if these early-entry routes are actually attracting individuals who would not otherwise have chosen to enter teaching. In our survey of teacher-preparation candidates in NYC, we find that very few of the early-entry candidates—only 8 percent of TFA candidates and 8 percent of NYCTF candidates—had also applied to traditional teacher-preparation programs, suggesting that the early-entry routes are attracting a different pool of teachers. We found that approximately one-fifth of individuals in traditional programs had also applied to early-entry programs, suggesting that there is a larger pool of traditional candidates who would have liked to attend the alternative routes but were not accepted. Feistritzer suggests that nearly half, 47 percent, would not have chosen to teach if they had not had an early-entry route available to them, and 25 percent of her sample indicated that they were not sure.[66] Less than one-quarter of her sample said they would have gone back to college and completed a traditional teacher-education program, and 6 percent would have found a job in a private school or in a setting in which they would not have to be certified.

Feistritzer also reports differences in this response by age, gender, and race. She suggests that the older one is, the less likely one is to enter teaching if an early-entry route is not available—lending credence to the argument that early-entry routes may be particularly appealing to older candidates:

> Nearly six out of 10 of those surveyed who were in their 50s or older when they entered an alternate route say they would not have become a teacher if an alternate route had not been available. Half of those in their 40s, 46 percent of those in their 30s and 45 percent of those in their 20s report they would not have become teachers if an alternate route had not been available. More than half of men entering teaching through alternate routes, compared to 45 percent of women, say they would not have become a teacher if an alternate route had not been available.[67]

She also reports that more candidates of color suggest they would not enter teaching if it were not for the opportunity to pursue a credential through an alternative route, noting that 53 percent of Hispanic teachers say they would not have become a teacher if an alternate route had not been available, compared to 48 percent of whites and 43 percent of African Americans. This finding suggests that early-entry pathways may attract a more diverse candidate into teaching than traditional pathways.

These studies do suggest a distinct attraction to early-entry programs for particular candidates. In addition, the appeal of alternative routes seems to rest upon convenience, ease of transition into teaching, and low costs. However, it is also important to note exceptions such as the TFA candidates in New York who were more persuaded by the reputation, program goals, and the potential for intellectual challenge, again suggesting the range of differences in populations of early-entry teachers. In addition, some studies suggest that bonuses are less important to some candidates than the opportunity to defray the costs of tuition and loss of salary. Finally, the current research also indicates that most early-entry candidates would not have chosen traditional routes, suggesting that the concern that these new routes into teaching pull candidates away from traditional programs may be unfounded.

WHERE ARE EARLY-ENTRY CANDIDATES CHOOSING TO TEACH?

According to the National Center for Education Statistics, of the twenty-two states that collect data on the types of communities where their early-entry participants teach, five states report that over 50 percent of their early-entry certification candidates teach in inner-city communities (California, District of Columbia, Maryland, Missouri, New York, Texas, and Utah).[68] Four states report that over 30 percent of their participants teach in small towns (Montana, Oklahoma, Oregon, and Texas). Only two states reported that over 30 percent of graduates teach in rural areas: Wyoming (100%) and Montana (50%). However, the remaining states did report a range of 2 to 21 percent of graduates choosing to teach in rural areas. Interestingly, eight states reported more than 30 percent of their graduates from early-entry programs were in suburban communities: Connecticut, Delaware, Maryland, Mississippi, Oklahoma, Oregon, Utah, and Vermont.

Feistritzer's study finds that many of the early-entry route respondents are teaching in large cities.[69] Half of survey respondents report they are teaching in a large city, 16 percent in a medium-sized city, 10 percent in a suburban area outside a central city, 10 percent in a small city, 8 percent in a rural area, and 6 percent in a small town.[70] Feistritzer suggests that early-entry certification candidates are much more likely to teach in a big city, noting:

> These results are compared to 14 percent of all teachers who teach in a large city and 15 percent who teach in a medium city, 15 percent in the suburbs, 13 percent in a small city, 17 percent in a small town and 26 percent in a rural area, according to survey now under way by the National Center for Education Information.[71]

She also reports that early-entry respondents in her sample are somewhat more willing to move within their state to a place where the demand for teaching is the greatest:

> Individuals entering teaching through alternate routes are slightly more inclined to move within state to teach where the demand for jobs is greatest than they are to move out of state. Thirty-one percent say that it is very likely or somewhat likely that they would move to a rural area within the state if demand for teachers were great; 36 percent say it is very likely or somewhat likely that they would move to a large metropolitan area within the state. Thirty-one percent indicate they would be very or somewhat likely to move to a metropolitan area out of state and 22 percent say they would be very or somewhat likely to move to a rural area out of state if the demand for teachers warranted such a move.[72]

With regard to TTT, Feistritzer reports that more than half of them are teaching in large cities (55%) or medium cities (31%).[73]

On the other hand, not all studies find that early-entry candidates end up teaching in the communities that need those teachers the most. For instance, Fowler, who studied the MINT program, found that less than half of the two thousand candidates recruited chose to teach in the thirteen high-needs districts targeted by the state.[74] He concluded that the program did not meet its goals of recruiting and retaining highly qualified teachers for the high-needs communities.

Recent research suggests that geography matters to new teachers, and this finding has important implications for recruiting early entrants as well as to where they may choose to teach after completing their programs. These studies have helped illuminate the role that geography can play in teachers' choices of where to teach.[75] Work by Boyd, Lankford, Loeb, and Wyckoff reveals that most teachers in New York State take jobs very close to their hometowns (the towns in which they attended high school).[76] They found that 61 percent of teachers entering teaching from 1999–2002 took a job within only fifteen miles of their hometown. Eighty-five percent took jobs within forty miles of their hometowns. These findings held true for both older teachers (born before 1963) and younger teachers (84.6% and 84.8% respectively). Similarly, Reininger finds that these patterns are not unique to New York and hold up on a national level as well.[77] Relatedly, Johnson and colleagues found that one of the major draws candidates described regarding early-entry programs was the relative convenience of the program—the degree to which the program was designed to be close to where candidates lived and worked.[78] However, not all studies consistently find that teachers prefer to remain close to their roots. For instance, Feistritzer found that nearly two-thirds of the candidates in her sample were not teaching within 150 miles of where they were born.[79]

CONCLUSIONS AND POLICY IMPLICATIONS

This review of the current literature on early-entry candidates and programs suggests that early entrants are a different population than those entering through traditional pathways. Indeed, it seems that many candidates who selected early-entry programs may have not entered teaching had early-entry programs not been available. These findings are particularly important in that they allay concerns that early-entry pathways could be pulling candidates away from traditional routes into teaching.

This review also suggests that in some key ways, early-entry pathways have been able to recruit the kinds of individuals into teaching that they have been designed to attract. For instance, current research suggests that these candidates are not only more diverse, but may also be slightly more likely to be male, than those candidates who enter teaching through more-traditional programs and pathways. Two studies also suggested that these candidates bring more linguistic diversity than traditional candidates; however, this characteristic has rarely been examined in research on early entrants. The research also suggests that these candidates may also be more likely to bring some unexpected and useful qualifications in terms of specific teaching and classroom experiences, than has been previously assumed.

On the other hand, our review does not suggest that early-entry programs consistently attract a more highly academically prepared individual. Nor is it clear that these candidates bring stronger subject-matter background or more substantial work experience (although research on these candidates' subject-matter knowledge and background is particularly thin). Thus, while early-entry programs are attracting some candidates with some highly sought qualifications, in some substantial ways they have failed to attract candidates with the most desirable mix of academic preparation, prior skills, work experience, expertise, and content knowledge.

However, some important exceptions exist. Programs that aim to recruit specific populations of teachers seem particularly effective in obtaining particular kinds of individuals. For instance, programs that were designed to appeal to elite, high-achieving students from strong academic institutions (such as Teach For America) did obtain candidates with such backgrounds. Programs such as MMTEP aimed at paraprofessionals who were already working within the public school system obtained candidates who had experience in the local school system, and planned to remain teaching in the system.[80] Indeed, targeting populations of candidates seems to represent an effective strategy for such programs. However, research done by Johnson and her colleagues found that not all early-entry programs are as purposeful in their recruitment, and hence, the candidates in their programs may represent a much broader range in terms of their commitments, background, and prior educational preparation.[81]

Our review suggests that the economics of preparation and teaching are key factors in candidates' decision to enter through an early-entry program. Efforts to keep tuition low and to alleviate some of the opportunity costs of teaching are particularly important features that appealed to many candidates. Interestingly, some of the research suggests that signing bonuses and other one-time incentives may be less important to candidates than assistance with the costs of preparation, such as tuition fees and the loss of salary (as well as the loss of future salary increases). However, some candidates expressed very different factors in their decisionmaking—for instance, the TFA candidates in New York described choosing the program based on its reputation, goals, and intellectual challenge—again underscoring the differences within the population of early-entry teachers.

In sum, our research suggests that early-entry programs have not been completely successful in recruiting the kind of individuals most hoped for to these programs. While the programs do seem to attract a slightly more diverse population, it seems possible that early-entry programs could be more purposeful in this regard. And, while some programs attract highly academically pre-pared candidates, not all do so as successfully. And finally, not all programs seem as effective in appealing to true mid-career, profes-sional candidates.

This suggests several implications for those teacher educators who are responsible for early-entry programs, and for policymak-ers interested in those programs. Because programs that are clear about the kinds of candidates they seek seem to be able to get them, this research suggests that in order to be more effective, early-entry programs should design targeted recruitment efforts. To capital-ize upon the interests of new teachers in entering nearby programs and teaching close to home, early-entry programs should factor in teacher's preferences for geographic proximity when considering where to recruit and prepare candidates. Furthermore, if teacher educators were to assess the needs of nearby districts, in terms of the specific populations of teachers they seek (such as special edu-cation teachers, math or science teachers), teacher educators could more purposefully match local needs. Such directed efforts can assist in much more strategic development and maintenance of local teaching labor markets.

In turn, teacher educators may be able to make use of the recent research on profiles of early-entry candidates that move beyond discrete characteristics, in order to identify potential candidates. Understanding more about the motivations, perceptions of teach-ing, and future plans of different candidates may be particularly important in developing these more-effective and specific recruit-ment efforts. For instance, knowing that the population of young college graduates that applies to TFA is heavily influenced by pro-gram mission and by the potential intellectual experience they might have, could help programs that may wish to attract more of such candidates. And, given that TFA reports that it receives 18,000 applications for only 2,900 positions, this pool of candidates may represent a potentially rich source of candidates who could be attracted to other early-entry programs with similar aims and goals.[82]

Policymakers should help guide teacher educators' recruitment efforts by supporting schools and districts in determining their specific needs. Furthermore, given that early-entry candidates are in no way a monolithic group, they should help develop and support a broader range of incentives that may appeal to different populations. While they should continue to fund early-entry programs that are low-cost, they could also consider a wider array of incentives, ranging from tuition reimbursement or waivers for younger early-entrant candidates who might be recent college graduates, to assistance with child-care costs or salary loss for those who might be career changers or older entrants with families. Supporting the development of some programs that have strong missions and goals, as well as rich educational content, may also help appeal to the large population of recent graduates who may be considering teaching as a first career. Such efforts may more effectively and purposefully support a broad range of early-entry candidates, helping them address key concerns and giving them a sense of certainty when they choose teaching as a profession.

The authors contributed equally to this chapter.

CHAPTER 3

Getting Beyond the Label: What Characterizes Alternative Certification Programs?

Daniel C. Humphrey and Marjorie E. Wechsler

Alternative teacher certification has become an increasingly common part of the teacher-preparation system. First established in the 1980s as a response to projected teacher shortages, alternative certification programs are found now in nearly every state and many colleges and universities.[1] More recently, school districts have begun their own teacher-preparation programs, often in partnership with local universities. In some parts of the country, nearly as many teachers enter the profession through alternative routes as traditional routes.[2] Despite its expansion, there is little agreement about what constitutes alternative certification. This chapter looks closely at seven alternative certification programs that represent a range of structures and approaches in order to determine the utility of the label, *alternative certification*.

Alternative certification is the form of teacher preparation that seems to defy definition and generate heated debates. Confusion about the meaning of such terms as *alternative routes* and *alternative certification* abounds. Some states deem any postbaccalaureate teacher-education program an alternative program, whereas other states consider this the traditional route. Some states use the term *alternative certification* for programs that employ teachers as teachers of record before they complete training. Also included under *alternative certification* are emergency permits carrying minimal requirements; national programs such as Teach For America; and the American Board for Certification of Teacher Excellence (ABCTE). Further complicating matters, some people differentiate between the terms *alternative certification* and *alternative route*— e.g., alternative certification involves reduced training for entry into teaching, whereas alternative routes are pathways other than four-year undergraduate or one-year postbaccalaureate programs that enable candidates to meet the same standards—and others use the terms interchangeably.

While our research cannot clear up confusion over terminology, it does closely examine seven alternative certification programs and their participants in order to better understand the variations in program structures and participants' experiences. In doing so, we challenge the usefulness of trying to characterize alternative certification. Instead, we argue for a new conception of teacher education that is less focused on programs, and contend that a better unit of analysis is the particular combination of an individual's educational preparation, work and teaching experience, preparation program including mentoring actually received, and the school environment where they begin teaching.

In the remainder of this chapter, we first present a brief description of the methods employed in our study. Next, we examine the structures of the programs and highlight the variation across the seven case-study programs. We then examine the characteristics of alternative certification participants, recognizing that variations in background impact how they experience their programs. We conclude the chapter with a discussion of the implications of these findings for both alternative and traditional teacher preparation.

STUDY METHODS

The research presented here is based on a three-year study of alternative certification. We employed multiple data-collection activities, focusing on seven alternative certification programs. For each program, we conducted interviews with key personnel three times over the course of the study. Respondents included the program director, teaching faculty, certification advisors, classroom supervisors, and others. We also collected and examined program documents, including program descriptions, course syllabi, existing evaluations or evidence of effectiveness, and other documents.

For each program, we surveyed participants at the beginning and end of their first year in the program. The survey included questions about participants' background, perceptions of preparedness for teaching, reasons for going into teaching, and reasons for choosing the alternative certification program. The questionnaire also measured participants' knowledge for teaching reading and mathematics, program supports received, career plans, and perceptions of growth.[3] In each program, we followed ten to thirteen participants as they progressed through the first year of their program. We conducted in-depth interviews and observed each participant in the classroom twice—once in the fall and again in the spring—using a structured observation instrument to measure the classroom learning environment, the teacher's pedagogical strategies, and classroom management. We also conducted interviews with other individuals influential to the participant's development as a teacher, including the principal and coaches or mentors who worked closely with the participant.

To ensure that the programs we studied met certain practical and theoretical criteria, we used a purposive sampling strategy that considered program scale, replicability, intensity of support, and participant characteristics. The seven programs are:

1. Teacher Education Institute (TEI) in the Elk Grove, California, Unified School District;
2. New Jersey's Provisional Teacher Program;
3. Milwaukee's Metropolitan Multicultural Teacher Education Program (MMTEP);
4. New York City Teaching Fellows Program (NYCTFP);
5. North Carolina's NC TEACH (North Carolina Teachers of Excellence for All Children);
6. Teach For America; and
7. Texas Region XIII Education Service Center's Educator Certification Program.

In six of the seven programs, participants are full-time teachers while completing their credential requirements. Elk Grove's Teacher Education Institute, which requires a full year of student teaching in concert with course work, is the exception. The programs vary in size and the targeted participant population. Milwaukee's MMTEP program is quite small, serving only twenty participants, all of whom have been paraprofessionals or teacher's aides in Milwaukee for at least one year. In contrast, the New York City Teaching Fellows Program prepares several thousand teachers annually, all of whom have strong academic and/or professional backgrounds. NC TEACH was designed to support mid-career professionals interested in switching to a career in education. New Jersey's Provisional Teacher Program trains teachers already hired to work as the teacher of record in schools. Teach For America recruits new college graduates from selective universities to serve as teachers in hard-to-staff urban and rural districts. The Texas

Region XIII Educator Certification Program targets both mid-career professionals and recent college graduates in high-need subject areas. All seven programs provide course work, though the focus and amount varies, as does the developer and provider of the course work. All seven programs also offer some type of mentoring, though the source and focus of mentoring varies. The one characteristic common to all programs is that they are considered to be alternative, rather than traditional, teacher-preparation programs.[4] A summary of each program is presented in exhibit 1.

CHARACTERIZING ALTERNATIVE CERTIFICATION PROGRAMS

Hawley's early critique of alternative certification research noted that studies failed to distinguish among different types of alternative certification programs.[5] Although individual studies may offer some insight into different program elements, little research has been conducted to fully describe program components or to compare the components across programs.[6] Much recent research continues to provide only cursory descriptions of program components. These descriptions, however superficial, provide the basis for many people's understandings of the type of training provided under the auspices of alternative certification.

In this section, we provide an in-depth view of the training provided through alternative certification programs. We explore the duration of programs, examining how long it takes for participants to complete the programs, how long it takes before participants serve as teachers of record, and how much course work is required. We also explore the clinical practice component, examining both how much clinical practice is required before participants become teachers of record and the quality of the clinical experience. We then describe the content of the course work. Finally, we explore the vagaries of teacher training when it occurs "on the job," look-

EXHIBIT 1
Program Summaries

Program	Stated Purpose(s)	Entrance Requirements	Primary Program Components	Number of participants
New Jersey's Provisional Teacher Program	• To allow career changers and other talented individuals streamlined access to the teaching profession • To eliminate the need to hire emergency teachers	• 2.75 minimum GPA • Major in subject • Passing score on the Praxis II subject-assessment test or National Teacher Examination specialty-area test	*Preservice:* • Individuals obtain a certificate of eligibility authorizing them to seek a teaching position • Once individual accepts an offer with a school, the state issues a provisional license • Pilot program offers 40 hours of preservice training *In-service:* • 200 hours of training offered at regional centers • Evaluation by district three times, the last of which includes a recommendation for standard licensure • Full-time mentor for initial 20-day period; continued mentor support for next 30 weeks	2,800

Program	Goals	Admission requirements	Program components	Number
Texas Region XIII Education Service Center's Educator Certification Program	• To recruit mid-career professionals and recent college graduates in high-need subject areas	• 2.5 overall GPA or 2.75 in last 60 semester hours • Competency in reading, writing, and math shown through test records, college course work, or master's degree • Required course work and semester hours in desired area • Online interview • Professional references • Daily computer access	*Preservice:* • Courses offered online and at the Region XIII training center in the spring • 2-week field experience *In-service:* • Continued course work • School-based mentors who are trained by Region XIII • Program-based field supporters	300
Milwaukee's Metropolitan Multicultural Teacher Education Program	• To provide urban children living in poverty with effective teachers • To recruit and prepare minority teachers • To prepare teachers who will remain in the Milwaukee system	• At least 1 year as a Milwaukee paraprofessional or teacher's aide • Interviews by Milwaukee Public Schools and University of Wisconsin-Milwaukee • Admissible as postbaccalaureate student in university's school of education	*Preservice:* • 6 weeks of course work and summer school teaching • Must receive positive evaluation to continue in program • University classes *In-service:* • Weekly university classes • Minimum of weekly visits by full-time mentors • Regular evaluations by supervisors	20

Program	Stated Purpose(s)	Entrance Requirements	Principal Program Components	Number of Participants
New York City Teaching Fellows Program	• To fill vacancies in New York City's lowest-performing schools	• 3.0 minimum GPA • Interview event comprised of a sample lesson, discussions of education articles, responses to classroom issues, and one-on-one interview	*Preservice:* • 8 weeks of master's degree course work provided by local public and private colleges and universities, field placement, and meetings with an advisor *In-service:* • Master's degree course work • Mentor provided by schools • Monthly mentor provided by university	2,600
NC TEACH	• To support mid-career professionals who want to switch to a career in education	• 2.5 minimum cumulative GPA • Degree with a major in, or relevant to, desired licensure area • At least 3 years of full-time work experience	*Preservice:* • Orientation • 5 week summer institute of full-time course work offered at 13 University of North Carolina campuses *In-service:* • Continued course work, advisement, and support • Mentor assigned by local education agency	452

Program	Goals	Requirements	Training	Number
Teach For America	• To close the achievement gap by providing teachers to underresourced schools and producing future leaders committed to closing the achievement gap	• 2.5 cumulative grade point average • Exhibit certain characteristics (have records of achievement and commitment to TFA mission, accept responsibility for outcomes, demonstrate organizational ability, show respect for others, possess critical thinking skills)	*Preservice:* • Assigned readings, structured teacher observations, follow-up conversations with observed teachers • 5-week summer training • 1- to 2-week orientation in placement region *In-service:* • Participants attend a certification program offered by a local university or other credentialing program • Ongoing support from the TFA regional office (learning teams, observations with feedback, workshops, discussion groups, "all corps" meetings)	1,800
Teacher Education Institute—Elk Grove (CA)	• To meet the growing district's need for credentialed teachers • To increase teacher quality by training teachers in the district's curriculum and practices	• 2.5 minimum GPA	*Preservice:* • 80 hours of course work • Classroom observations *In-service:* • Course work • Internship in classroom of a "master teacher coach"—16 hours per week in fall, 4 days per week in spring	100

ing at the impact of school context on participants' training and the nature and quality of mentoring provided.

Duration of Alternative Certification Programs

Although many describe alternative certification programs as "fast-track," that designation does not apply universally to all programs. The programs we studied ranged considerably in duration. Four of the seven programs, for example, involve yearlong preparation; the Texas Region XIII program lasts for about a year and half; and the New York City Teaching Fellows Program requires two years of training. Alternative routes, thus, do not necessarily expedite credentialing. However, alternative certification expedites the process of an individual becoming the teacher of record (i.e., the individual is the teacher with sole responsibility for a classroom). Among the seven case-study sites, the most common program structure includes summer course work with some small amount of clinical practice, followed in the fall with the placement of the participant as the teacher of record in a classroom with mentoring support and continued course work. All but two of the case-study programs mirror this approach. MMTEP, for example, begins in June with its six-week summer component. During this time, participants take course work and participate in preservice clinical training, serving as student teachers in a summer school. After successful completion of the summer component, participants begin the school year in the fall as the teachers of record in a Milwaukee Public School classroom. During the school year, participants continue to attend weekly classes, meet weekly with their mentor, and undergo formal evaluation on a periodic basis.

Not all alternative certification programs follow this popular design, however. Two of the case-study programs provide a contrast in the amount of time required in the program before participants serve as teachers of record. The New Jersey program offers the quickest time to become a teacher of record. In fact, this program requires that teachers have a teaching position before enrolling in the program. Thus, a participant can become a teacher of record before receiving any preparation whatsoever. Teacher Education Institute (TEI) in Elk Grove, on the other hand, requires a full academic year of course work and field experience before participants assume responsibility for their own classrooms. In practice, TEI participants receive substantially more clinical experience than teachers in most traditional preparation programs.

The programs also varied considerably with regard to earning a credential. When course work alone is considered, the seven programs require significantly different numbers of credit hours. The New Jersey program, for example, requires the completion of 200 hours of course work, far fewer than the approximately 400 to 500 hours required in New Jersey's traditional university programs. Clearly this is a fast-track program. In contrast, participants in the New York City Teaching Fellows Program must complete the same number of graduate credits as those pursuing a traditional master's degree. This approach does not appear to fit the definition of "fast-track."

In sum, there is no single approach to how and when alternative certification programs streamline the process of becoming a teacher. Although programs rarely lead to faster full certification, they do, often, place participants in classrooms faster. Other requirements like course work, however, vary from program to program.

Extent of Clinical Practice

As described above, many programs place alternative certification teachers in classrooms before completing their training; however, nearly all of the alternative certification programs include some clinical training prior to participants becoming teachers of record. As with other programmatic aspects, though, the length and the quality of that training vary considerably.

TEI in Elk Grove provides the longest and most intensive clinical training. As we noted earlier, TEI expects participants to complete a year of largely field-based training before they become responsible for their own classrooms. Participants in the TEI program complete two practicums, one each in the fall and spring. Participants working toward an elementary-level credential receive placements in one Title I and one non–Title I school, and have one experience in the primary elementary grades and another in the upper elementary grades. The program places those working toward secondary certification in a middle school during the summer and in another assignment during the school year. A master teacher coach—an experienced faculty member selected by the district—guides and supervises the practicum by issuing a series of responsibilities in slow progression.

Although TEI differs from the other alternative certification programs we studied, a careful look at all seven programs suggests that alternative certification programs typically have some form of preservice clinical practice, albeit in a truncated form. As exhibit 2 suggests, most of the programs offer only a limited amount of clinical practice. Alternative route teachers in six of the seven programs received clinical practice lasting six weeks or less. In contrast, traditional teacher candidates typically receive eight to twelve weeks of clinical practice in addition to as many as 100 hours of classroom experiences prior to their clinical practice.

Of course, program descriptions do not necessarily reflect the actual experiences of program participants. Participants did not always receive the program as designed. Not all TEI participants, for example, actually receive a full year of clinical practice. In some cases, program participants became the teacher of record when

EXHIBIT 2
Preservice Clinical Experience Required, by Program

Program	*Clinical Practice Required Before Becoming a Teacher of Record*
MMTEP	6 weeks half-time during summer school
NC TEACH	Classroom observations only
New Jersey Program	4 weeks of coteaching with a mentor
New York City Teaching Fellows	Some opportunities during summer school
TFA	4 weeks during the summer
TEI, Elk Grove	1 year
Texas Region XIII	2 weeks during summer school

an opening occurred before program completion. Similarly, New Jersey program participants are supposed to spend their first four weeks working with a full-time mentor, a form of clinical practice. However, the reality is that a full-time mentor is rarely available. Instead, participants typically have a mentor who is also teaching his/her own class full-time or is a part-time retired teacher.

The quality of the participants' clinical practice also depends on the skill of the supervising teacher. As with traditional teacher education, student teaching can be a rewarding and educational experience when the master teacher possesses the proper instructional skills and understands how to impart that knowledge to other adults. Some master teachers, however, do not exhibit quality teaching; or if they do, they may be unable to articulate to the novice tacit knowledge about instruction and classroom management.

The quality of participants' clinical practice also depends on the timing of the placement. In New York City and Milwaukee, for example, alternative certification participants complete their clinical preservice training during summer school. These summer school experiences do expose the participants to students and classrooms, but both programs acknowledge important differences in summer school from the regular academic year, including differences in the student populations served, class sizes (summer school classes are often smaller), and even the curriculum. Thus, preservice during the summer may not be ideal for preparing teachers for the regular school year.

As will be discussed later, however, large numbers of alternative certification program participants enter their programs with experience as a classroom teacher, teacher's aide, or substitute teacher. In some of those cases, participants' previous teaching experiences could be thought of as significant clinical experience.

In sum, both the quantity and the quality of the clinical practice that alternative certification teachers receive vary, both by design and by circumstance. There is no single description that could represent the clinical experiences provided by alternative certification programs.

Alternative Certification Course Work

Both alternative certification and traditional teacher preparation provide training through course work. Like the other program components discussed thus far, however, alternative certification course work varies in the emphasis placed on subject-matter content, pedagogy, classroom management, and child development. These variations exist not only among different programs but also within individual programs as well.

Some programs primarily focus on preparing graduates to work with the specific curricula of the school districts in which their graduates teach. TEI in Elk Grove is one such program. Although TEI offers a broad array of courses, it also focuses specifically on district adoptions. And, when the adoptions change, so too do the instructional approaches that TEI teaches. TEI used to teach a language development model of reading instruction, for example. When the district switched to Open Court, a phonics-based reading series, TEI began emphasizing phonics. MMTEP, likewise, has developed its own curriculum, which although emphasizing a wide range of topics, is designed to meet the specific needs of teachers in the Milwaukee Public Schools and is tailored to its participants who are already familiar with Milwaukee's classrooms and students. In fact, many times throughout the course, Milwaukee district administrators serve as guest lecturers for particular topics. Moreover, because of the small number of participants and because a single person designs the course work, the curriculum can be revised in mid-course to accommodate participants' strengths and weaknesses and areas that need further development.

In contrast, some programs emphasize educational foundations and theory, and the content resembles that of traditional teacher-education programs. University-based programs tend to center their course work on the regular preparation program offered through those institutions. A sixty-five-member panel comprised of university faculty and master teachers from across the state, for example, developed NC TEACH's 5,000-page curriculum document, which frames a series of modules. Although organized in a way to address the needs of the program participants, the document covers much of the same content as the traditional university programs, albeit in a condensed time frame. All thirteen host universities use the NC TEACH curriculum.

In contrast, each of the host universities of the New York City Teaching Fellows program designs its own course work for the Fellows. Because they are pursuing master's degrees, Fellows take a range of courses; however, specific course work varies across the colleges and universities. Most borrow directly from their traditional training programs, simply tailoring the schedule to meet the needs of the working Fellows by offering evening and weekend classes. Exceptions apply, however. Some colleges departed from their traditional teacher-preparation curricula to develop specific courses for the Fellows. One college, for example, focuses on the district's adopted curriculum. Another operates a much more personalized program with a flexible curriculum, designed to meet the needs of teachers learning on the job.

As with other program components, then, course work varies within and across programs. Some alternative certification participants receive course work that is primarily theoretical, while others receive course work that is primarily practical.

On-the-Job Training

With the vast majority of alternative certification participants serving as the teacher of record in a classroom, they are learning to teach on the job. To supplement the field-based learning, alternative certification programs often include a mentoring component through which an experienced teacher provides guidance and support to the novice teacher. Although typically not controlled by the program, school context and the quality of the mentoring affect the on-the-job training offered to new teachers, either enhancing or impeding program efforts.

School Context

Because alternative certification participants learn on the job, they learn not only from their program but also from their colleagues and administrators as well. Both the formal and informal aspects of schools influence their development. Formally, as members of a school community, alternative certification teachers participate in professional development programs provided by the school or district. The teaching strategies introduced or reinforced through

these formal learning opportunities often focus on a particular curriculum or instructional approach adopted by a district or school,
such as Readers' or Writers' Workshops in many New York City
Schools or the Open Court reading series in Elk Grove Unified
School District. Because formal school- or district-based professional development and alternative certification programs operate
independently of one another, the extent to which their educational philosophies and teaching strategies correspond is most often
coincidental rather than a consequence of design. As a result, the
theories of teaching and learning and the instructional strategies
that alternative certification participants learn from the different
sources may cohere or, perhaps more importantly, may conflict.

More opportunity for coherence between school-based professional development and the alternative certification training exists
in programs sponsored and created by districts, which by design
focus both their professional development and alternative certification training on preparing graduates to work with the district
curricula. Thus, what participants learn in their alternative certification program and what they learn in their school-based professional development reinforce each other. Although beneficial in its
coherence, this focused approach is limiting to teachers who may
someday work in another district or with a different curriculum.

For alternative certification programs that serve multiple districts, such coordination is not feasible. For example, because NC
TEACH is located at thirteen host institutions across the state, the
program adapts more to regional educational needs, but not necessarily to those of the local districts. The Texas Region XIII program
has participants working in forty-four districts, making it impossible for the program to address particular district curricula. Further complicating matters, the districts it serves range from highly
traditional to more reform-oriented districts. As a result, different sources of training do, at times, present different approaches

to instruction. In the best case, the lessons from the different providers reinforce each other; in the worst case, they contradict each other. We have seen examples of both. One participant in the Texas Region XIII program said that she does not try to mix what she learns from her alternative certification program and her district's professional development academy, noting, "It will get confusing."

Having control over participants' learning and ensuring coherence not only create problems for larger alternative certification programs or programs serving multiple districts, but doing so can also be problematic for programs serving individual districts. The case of MMTEP—our smallest case-study program and a program serving a single district—illustrates how each participant may learn completely different instructional strategies as a result of his or her school placement. The Milwaukee Public Schools operate in a highly decentralized environment, with each school determining its core philosophy or approach to education. As members of unique school communities, MMTEP participants learn quite different ways to teach. We observed one teacher in a direct-instruction school teach literacy by following a script. In contrast, another participant in a Paideia school—a model that emphasizes active learning through didactic instruction, coaching of academic skills, and seminar discussion—worked with literature circles. Although both attended the same certification program, what the participants learned about teaching reading was based to a great degree on their schools' philosophies and curricular adoptions, not on their formal certification classes.

The informal school context also plays a large role in participants' development. The school environments in which alternative certification participants work vary to such a great extent that it is difficult to determine whether on-the-job learning is advantageous or not. Some participants experience rich and supportive environments in which they thrive and learn their new profession; others experience chaotic and unsupportive environments that not only prevent them from learning how to teach, but also drive them from the profession. Two schools in the same urban district provide contrasting examples of the different environments where alternative certification teachers work. Both schools served highly diverse student populations and high percentages of low-achieving students. Although the schools had similar student bodies, the workplace conditions of the two could not have been more different.

In one school, teachers received support for their instruction as well as their classroom management. The school assigns a mentor to work with all the new teachers, including those in the alternative certification program. The mentor—a highly successful, experienced teacher—met weekly with all new teachers as a group to share resources and materials, instructional strategies, and curriculum guidance. The school established a preparation period specifically for this meeting so the teachers did not have to spend time after school, nor did they have to sacrifice their regular preparation time. The mentor also observed the teachers conducting lessons and provided them with individualized support to meet their specific needs. Although serving a challenging population, a clear schoolwide discipline policy and support for enforcing it by the administrators assisted teachers with their classroom management. The tone set in the school kept discipline problems to a minimum, enabling teachers to focus primarily on instruction. Discipline problems still arose in the new teachers' classrooms, but they could call for assistance from the administrators. Teachers in this school reported feeling supported and having the help they needed to effectively run their classrooms and provide instruction.

In contrast, the other school provided neither classroom management nor instructional support. Although all new teachers in the district are supposed to be assigned a mentor, new teachers in this school were not. Little schoolwide professional community existed, and new teachers had to rely on one another for instructional and moral support rather than on their more experienced colleagues. The school also experienced extreme discipline problems. Students roamed the hallways during class periods, teachers could be heard yelling at students, and fights among students occurred regularly. The new teachers had nowhere to go for help; administrators reprimanded new teachers who asked for assistance with unruly students. The new teachers in this school focused on merely surviving each day, not on learning the teaching profession.

Alternative certification may be based on the theory of on-the-job training, but we found little attention paid at the program level to where that training should occur. As the examples above demonstrate, alternative certification teachers may be placed in a school with a supportive administration and a professional learning community in which they can grow and develop into strong professionals. Or they may be placed in a school so dysfunctional that they are driven from teaching before they even complete their programs. They may be assigned to a grade-level team that works together, sharing materials and ideas for lessons. Or, they may be isolated from the rest of the staff, finding themselves with no colleagues from whom to learn. On-the-job training in and of itself thus does not sufficiently guarantee a strong teacher-development program. Because learning occurs on the job, participants have very different learning opportunities both across and within programs, again making it difficult to characterize alternative certification.

Quality Mentoring

Complementing the on-the-job training, all seven programs provide mentoring to support their participants. But mentoring, like other training components, varies considerably across and within programs, not just in terms of the amount of mentoring provided, but in its quality as well. Some programs, like the Texas Region XIII program, provide training for mentors, but most programs do not. Some programs, like MMTEP, have full-time mentors, whereas others rely on volunteers who already have full-time jobs as classroom teachers. In addition, the content of the mentoring varies. Some mentors see their jobs as primarily providing emotional support; others keep the focus on instructional strategies. Only a few programs have a set curriculum for mentors to follow. With a few exceptions, we found a lack of quality control over mentors' work. As a result, some alternative certification teachers received excellent mentoring, while others did not.

Additionally, in some instances, alternative certification participants had two mentors—one from the alternative certification program, and one from the school or district, provided through an induction program. Again, learning from two sources can be either reinforcing or contradictory. In the New York City program, for example, Fellows are assigned both university- and school-based mentors. University faculty expressed concerns that the different mentors might provide conflicting advice. The degree of coherence may reflect the amount of training and supervision provided to either set of mentors.

Our observations of and interviews with teachers across the seven programs clearly indicated that when an alternative certification teacher with a solid set of teaching skills and a reasonable teaching assignment receives quality mentoring, the participant can succeed. However, when the quality of the mentoring is lacking, teaching skills are weak, and the teaching assignment is difficult, the alternative certification teacher struggles.

In sum, our analysis of alternative certification programs establishes that these programs defy simplistic characterizations. A review of the design of the seven case-study programs suggests that nearly all programs include some preservice clinical training, although the length and the quality of that training vary. Some programs may be described as fast-track into the classroom, while others are quite lengthy. Alternative certification course work varies, both across and within programs, in its emphasis on subject-matter content, pedagogy, classroom management, and child development. Although on-the-job training is emphasized, alternative certification programs frequently offer participants on-the-job training that is unpredictable. Too often, the course work offered by the program is contradicted by the on-the-job training at the school. Further, because market forces drive the teachers' placements, the alternative certification program rarely guarantees a match between the participants' training needs and the kinds of supports available at the school. Mentoring is a key component of every program we examined; however, programs rarely take care to guarantee the quality and effectiveness of that mentoring support.

PROGRAM PARTICIPANTS AND PROGRAM STRUCTURES

Our examination of program structures illustrates the variation of approaches across programs and the difficulty of characterizing alternative certification programs. Further complicating matters, our analysis revealed that individual participant characteristics shaped how they experienced those program structures. Ultimately, it is *how* participants experience their programs that matters most. Thus, we examined the variation in participants' backgrounds in order to better understand the interaction between programs as designed and participants' experiences in these programs. First we look at the demographics of participants and establish that these participants are quite different than popular assumptions assume. We then look at the educational backgrounds of participants, and, finally, at their prior professional experiences.

The Demographics of Alternative Certification Participants

Demographically, alternative certification teachers in our sample are a very diverse group; however, they are not very different from traditional-route teachers. While the mean age of participants is slightly higher than teachers in traditional preparation programs, the age range within programs is considerably wide, with alternative certification teachers representing both older individuals as well as new college graduates. Further, national data and data from the seven case-study programs indicate no considerable gender differences between alternative certification and traditional preparation participants. Some individual programs, however, do attract greater percentages of men to the teaching profession than national averages.

Alternative certification programs are sometimes designed to diversify the pool of new teachers, and overall averages suggest that they are successful in attracting greater percentages of minorities into the teaching profession. However, program participants tend to reflect the racial composition of their local labor market.[7] Only Milwaukee's MMTEP program was successful in attracting a significantly higher percentage of minority teachers than the local labor market.

Education Backgrounds of Alternative Certification Participants

The case-study programs included individuals with a variety of educational backgrounds. Some of the programs attract significant numbers of individuals who attended competitive colleges and universities, whereas others do not. The percentage of participants who attended a competitive undergraduate institution reflects the recruitment priorities of the program; some specifically recruit highly educated individuals (e.g., Teach For America), while others

EXHIBIT 3
Percentage of Participants Who Attended Competitive Undergraduate Universities, by Program***

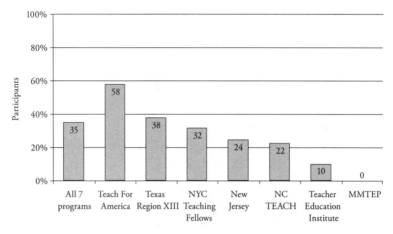

***p < .001.

Source: SRI Survey of Alternative Certification Program Participants (2003, 2004).

recruit individuals with experience in schools and a demonstrated commitment to the community (e.g., MMTEP).[8]

We used Barron's six-scale selectivity ranking for undergraduate universities and coded participants as having attended a competitive or a less competitive institution of higher education (IHE).[9] We included Barron's two highest rankings in our "competitive" category, and two lowest rankings in our "less competitive" category. Although alternative route teachers overall are more likely to have graduated from competitive universities than from less competitive ones, we found wide variation (see exhibit 3). The percentage of alternative certification participants attending a competitive college ranges from 58 percent of TFA participants to none of MMTEP's participants. Of course, the competitiveness of the college or university that an individual attended is just one indicator

EXHIBIT 4
Prior Careers of Alternative Certification Participants

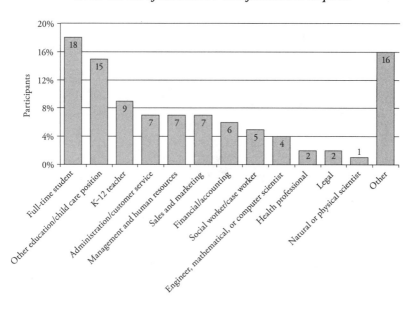

Source: SRI Survey of Alternative Certification Program Participants (2003, 2004).

of a well-educated individual, though research suggests that teachers with strong academic backgrounds may be more effective than less well-educated teachers.[10]

Alternative Certification Candidates' Previous Career and Classroom Experience

Although we did encounter some career changers with impressive professional backgrounds, more participants in the seven programs had been full-time students or employed in some education-related field. Exhibit 4 presents the prior careers of participants in the seven programs. Overall, relatively few participants—about 5 per-

EXHIBIT 5
Percentage of Participants with Some Classroom Experience***

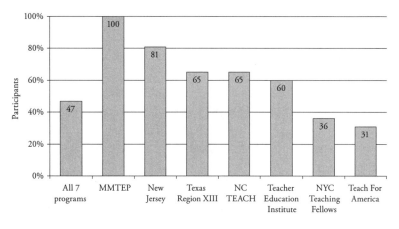

***p < .001.
Source: SRI Survey of Alternative Certification Program Participants (2003, 2004).

cent—switched from careers in mathematics and science to teaching; only 2 percent came from the legal profession; and 6 percent
came from a financial or accounting career. In contrast, about 42
percent of participants were either in education or were full-time
students immediately before entering their alternative certification
program. Accordingly, when we examined the financial changes
that participants made to enter the teaching profession, we found
that the majority of participants in the seven programs experienced
a salary increase.[11]

Perhaps most instructive to understanding alternative certification participants, nearly half of participants had classroom experience prior to entering their program. In five of the seven programs,
more than 60 percent of participants report having had previous
experience as a classroom teacher, substitute teacher, or teacher's
aide (see exhibit 5). Although further study about the quality of

their time spent working in classrooms needs to be undertaken, we were surprised not just by how many participants had prior classroom experience, but also by the length of those experiences. For example, New Jersey participants who had previous teaching experience averaged thirty-nine months of experience.[12] Similarly, 41 percent of participants across all seven programs had at least a full academic year of classroom experience.

These demographic and background variables provide just a small glimpse into alternative certification participants. Although we only describe a few variables here, they adequately demonstrate the complexities of thinking about alternative certification programs. Though we can make statements about alternative certification participants as a whole, means mask important variation both across and within programs. The variation matters, not just as a statistical exercise, but also because *who* participates matters to the supports they will need to develop into professional teachers. And, the variation matters because it impacts *how* they will experience those supports.

Paths to Teaching

Given the wide variation in program components and participant characteristics both within and across programs, characterizing alternative certification as a single entity becomes nearly meaningless. Instead, it is important to consider all of the factors that shape new teachers' development, for each factor influences the others. In addition to the program itself, it is important to consider two other important factors: the skills and experiences individuals bring to their programs, and the support they receive in their schools.[13] Specifically, teacher candidates' preparation and teaching ability are shaped by the interaction of their personal background (their academic background and previous classroom experiences), their formal training, (e.g., course work as experienced), and the context of their school placement (principal and mentor support, professional community, and availability of materials). These three factors—personal background, preparation, and school context—define the candidates' paths into the teaching profession.

Two teachers, Ms. H. and Mrs. W., illustrate how two teachers can have different learning experiences because of their own backgrounds, even when they are in the same alternative certification program and work in the same school. Ms. H. and Mrs. W. both work at the same urban elementary school, serving a primarily minority population of low-performing students. Ms. H. is twenty-three years old, quite young compared with other teachers in her program. She initially had difficulty gaining admission to the program, but was admitted when the program lowered the required grade point average. Ms. H.'s mother, herself a teacher, encouraged her to pursue the profession. Ms. H. worked in a variety of day-care centers and youth programs as she grew up. She also had experience in this school, serving for two years as a teacher's aide for a teacher reputed to be among the best in the school. In fact, when this teacher fell ill, Ms. H. ran the classroom by herself for two months. When Ms. H. finally took the helm of her own first-grade classroom, she had the confidence of an experienced teacher, the support of the other teachers with whom she had previously worked, and the support of her mother. She was energetic, eager to learn, and, importantly, not overwhelmed by her daily classroom experiences. Consequently, she was able to attend her evening credentialing classes ready to learn and to apply her new knowledge to her classroom the next day.

In contrast, Mrs. W. had no trouble gaining admission to the program. She was highly educated, having already earned an advanced degree, and having worked as a highly regarded business professional. In addition, Mrs. W. was deeply committed to the city and the community, as demonstrated by her volunteer work in the minority community in which she lived. But her experiences in the school were less than positive. As a foreign language teacher, Mrs. W. did not have her own classroom, and the principal used her to provide other teachers with release time. As a result, she pushed classroom materials from room to room on a cart. The school never assigned her a formal mentor, even though mentors were considered a key component of her alternative certification program; and she had trouble finding an informal mentor. Admitting to not knowing how to teach her subject or how to manage a classroom, she was isolated from other teachers and thus had no one from whom to learn. She found herself exhausted at the end of the day; and although she went to her credentialing classes at night, she was discouraged and enervated and had trouble applying what she learned to her situation.

Ms. H. and Mrs. W. came from quite different backgrounds and encountered different professional learning environments in the same school. Ms. H. was young with less formal education herself, but her prior classroom experiences, her connections to the other teachers in her school, and her family support gave her the tools she needed to run a successful classroom and to benefit from her course work. Mrs. W. was unable to find peer support in her school, had no prior experiences from which to draw, and struggled in her daily teaching activities.

The interaction of three factors—the program as implemented, the school context, and each participant's background—shape the learning experiences of individual participants, as demonstrated by the cases of Ms. H. and Mrs. W. Although Ms. H. had a weaker academic background than Mrs. W., Ms. H. found the course work in her program to be useful, in part, because she had already established a foundation of classroom management skills and basic knowledge of how to teach reading and mathematics. In contrast, despite her graduate degree, commitment to helping build the community, and successful professional career, Mrs. W. found little of her program helpful—in part, because her classroom responsibilities overwhelmed her during the day. Although they worked in the same school, Ms. H. enjoyed strong mentoring support, perhaps because she had worked as a classroom aide in the school; Mrs. W., on the other hand, felt isolated and at a loss for where to get help. In this case, the alternative certification program happened to be well matched to the trajectory Ms. H. had taken into the teaching profession and a disservice to Mrs. W. and her students. This example illustrates the importance of paths into teaching. Looking only at the program would miss important aspects of the two teachers' training. Examining the program in light of their backgrounds and school contexts, however, provides a more complete understanding of their teacher preparation.

CONCLUSIONS

In our examination of seven alternative certification programs, we discovered that there is more variation within a single preparation program than there is across programs in terms of the training teacher candidates are offered, the schools where they are placed, the supports they receive from the program and their school, and how they experience their preparation. Other research supports these findings and shows that the same within-program variation exists for both traditional and alternative certification programs. Boyd, Grossman, Lankford, Loeb, and Wyckoff, for example, examined the effects on student achievement of teachers from various teacher-preparation programs, including both traditional and alternative certification programs.[14] They found that, among other things, the variation in effectiveness within programs is far greater than the average difference between programs. Another recent study of the effectiveness of certified, uncertified, and alternatively certified teachers in the New York City public schools found little difference between routes in terms of student achievement, but found dramatic differences within routes.[15] When they ranked teachers by the value they added to student achievement, they found that the impact of assigning a student to a top-quartile teacher versus a bottom-quartile teacher was ten times the impact of assigning a student to a teacher with a particular kind of certification or from a particular program. Our own research also found more variation within programs than between programs in terms of teachers' knowledge of teaching reading and mathematics, teacher efficacy, planned retention, and reported growth.[16]

This broader conception of teacher preparation—one that emphasizes paths into the profession rather than programs—has important implications for the ongoing dialogue about how to prepare skilled teachers. Understanding the unique contributions of each component of a teacher's path into the profession, and the interaction of multiple components, becomes more important than the search for the perfect preparation program. Unfortunately, both researchers and policymakers are often fixated on program-level solutions to complex problems. The numerous "horse race" studies comparing student test scores of Teach For America (TFA) teachers and others are good examples of the problem. The studies inevitably declare a winner, but a closer look shows that the margin of victory is so small as to be nearly meaningless. What does it mean to find out that TFA teachers can move their students from the thirteenth to the fourteenth percentile in math?

Instead of investing millions of dollars in these program-to-program comparison studies, it would be wiser to fund research that attempts to understand the combination of factors—both personal and programmatic—that adds up to effective teaching. We currently know very little about how a teacher candidate's educational background, previous classroom experience, course work, clinical practice, mentoring, and school placement interact to produce a teacher with the skills and knowledge necessary to meet the academic needs of diverse students. The research will be difficult in and of itself. The real challenge, however, will be in applying this research to practice.

Attending to teacher candidates' paths into the profession has major implications for all forms of preparation programs, both alternative and traditional. At the very least, recognizing the importance of individual paths underscores the importance of assessing the skills and knowledge of teacher candidates early and often, and then tailoring a package of course work, clinical practice, mentoring, and appropriate placement to fit the needs of different individuals. This approach requires the difficult abandonment of a fixed set of program components in exchange for an assessment-based and individualized set of training and supports. Currently, neither traditional preparation nor alternative certification programs use the information they collect on their teacher candidates' skills and knowledge to tailor their programs to individuals' needs.

Our study found that some beginning teachers who entered teaching through an alternative certification program are effective beginning on their first day in the classroom. This existence proof runs counter to the widely held assumption that all new teachers must struggle through their first year. Raising the expectation that all teachers—whether prepared by alternative or traditional programs—are effective on day one is best realized by less emphasis on broad policy debates and more attention to the intricate combination of factors that add up to teacher effectiveness. Our research suggests that in order to realize the guarantee of day-one effectiveness, attention must be paid to the multiple components of a teacher candidate's path into the profession, along with an individualized and tailored program designed to address deficiencies in subject-matter knowledge, pedagogical skills, attitudes, and knowledge of teaching.

This research was made possible by a grant from Carnegie Corporation of New York. The statements made and views expressed are solely the responsibility of the authors.

For their many contributions to this paper, the authors would like to acknowledge the entire research team: Nancy Adelman, Katherine Baisden, Barnett Berry, Kristin Bosetti, Christopher Chang-Ross, H. Alix Gallagher, Heather Hough, Paul Hu, Harold Javitz, Dylan Johnson, Andrea Lash, John Luczak, Diana Montgomery, Tiffany Price, and Andrew Wayne. We would also like to thank Dan Fallon, Suzanne Wilson, and Ken Zeichner for their critical feedback. Finally, this research would not have been possible without the cooperation of the program staff, principals, and teachers in each of the seven programs studied. We are grateful for the time they contributed for interviews, and for allowing us to observe their work.

PART II

Outcomes of Alternative Certification Programs

CHAPTER 4

Is Fast-Track Preparation Enough? It Depends

Susan Moore Johnson and Sarah E. Birkeland

Teacher quality is the topic of the day in public education, with policymakers, school officials, teachers, and the public intensely debating who should be allowed to teach and what preparation they should have. Much of this debate centers on the effectiveness of "fast-track" alternative teacher certification programs, designed to attract strong candidates who otherwise might not enter teaching. These programs tend to be shorter, less expensive, more convenient, and more practically oriented than traditional university-based programs. Given their brevity, critics question whether such programs can effectively prepare candidates for the challenging work of classroom teaching.

Traditional teacher-preparation programs invest heavily in preservice training on the assumption that a rich and substantial set of courses and clinical experiences will give teachers what they need to succeed in the classroom. Alternative certification introduces a different approach to preparation, one in which teachers are expected to develop over time, and the process of acquiring knowledge and expertise is distributed across several stages of the teacher's career. Most of these programs depend minimally on preservice preparation, relying instead on the skills, knowledge, and life experience that candidates bring to teaching, as well as the ongoing support and professional development that new teachers will receive on the job. Thus, much of the responsibility for preparation shifts from the preservice program to school-based support.

Is the training provided by fast-track alternative certification programs adequate for teachers as they enter the classroom? This simple question has no simple answer, since there are so many interpretations of what "adequate" preparation means, so much variety in who these prospective teachers are, and such a range in what programs actually offer. Nonetheless, given the expanded use of alternative certification, it is an important question to investigate.

In 2002, we studied the experiences of eighty individuals participating in alternative certification programs at thirteen program sites in four states.[1] We asked these future teachers to assess the adequacy of their preparation on their own terms. By interviewing the participants twice, once during the program and again six to eight months later, we sought to understand whether they thought that their program provided sufficient foundation for their early months in the classroom. They had been attracted by the programs' intended incentives—brief, inexpensive, convenient, and practical training—which would allow them to move quickly into a teaching position and avoid the tuition and opportunity costs of longer preservice training in traditional programs. However, it became clear that success during the first year rested on far more than what the program provided. In the end, the new teachers' readiness for teaching depended not only on what their program offered, but also on the skills and experience they brought to their training and the support they received in their schools. Thus, we found that three elements—the person, the program, and the school—contributed to these teachers' sense of preparedness during the first year.

RESEARCH ABOUT TEACHER TRAINING
AND TEACHER QUALITY

Scholars have sought to assess and compare the relative success of teachers who completed alternative and traditional programs by using various indicators of teacher quality, including ratings by observers, student test scores, measures of subject-matter knowledge, and teachers' self-reported sense of efficacy.[2] We briefly examine each of these approaches.

Several small studies of local programs rely on principals' ratings to compare the efficacy of alternatively and traditionally certified teachers. The results of these studies have been mixed. For example, in 1996 James Jelmberg reviewed principals' ratings and concluded that alternatively certified teachers are less effective in the classroom than their traditionally certified counterparts. Martha Ovando and Mary Trube conducted a similar study in 2000 and reached the same conclusion. However, other studies by Edith Guyton and her colleagues in 1991 and John Miller and his colleagues in 1998 found no appreciable differences between principals' ratings of the two groups.[3]

Researchers who use student test scores to compare the quality of alternatively and traditionally certified teachers also report conflicting findings. Daniel Goldhaber and Dominic Brewer, who analyzed a national data set (National Education Longitudinal Study), reported in 2000 that students whose teachers hold a standard, probationary, or emergency license in math perform better than students whose teachers are not certified or hold private school certification. However, the authors stress that there is no significant difference in the performance of students whose teachers hold standard rather than emergency credentials. They assert that these results "strongly contrast with the conventional wisdom . . . that good teachers only come through conventional routes."[4] Ildiko Laczko-Kerr and David Berliner, on the other hand, concluded in 2000 that a teacher's certification status *does* matter. These authors found that the students of certified teachers outperformed the students of "undercertified" teachers by about two months on the grade-level equivalence scale in reading, math, and language arts.[5]

Several research teams have studied the performance of participants in Teach For America (TFA), a national organization that places recent liberal arts graduates without a teaching license in hard-to-staff schools. An experimental design study conducted in 2004 by Paul Decker, Daniel Mayer, and Steven Glazerman showed that TFA teachers had modest, positive effects on students' math scores when compared to those of their certified, experienced counterparts.[6] However, there was no difference in their reading scores. Soon after, however, Linda Darling-Hammond, Deborah Holtzman, Su Jin Gatlin, and Julian Heilig found that TFA teachers generated smaller student achievement gains than teachers with traditional certification.[7]

Some studies have found no significant difference between traditionally and alternatively certified teachers in the extent of their subject-matter knowledge. For example, in 1989 Parmalee Hawk and Mary Schmidt studied eighteen alternatively prepared (fast-track) and eighteen traditionally prepared teachers in North Carolina and found no differences among the two groups in their scores on tests of content knowledge; they also found no differences in scores among those who majored in the disciplines tested and those who did not. In studying the mathematical knowledge of fifty-five alternate route teachers who had math degrees, G. Williamson McDiarmid and Suzanne Wilson found in 1991 that these teachers commonly understood mathematical algorithms, but not the underlying mathematical theory or concepts.[8]

Megan Tschannen-Moran, Anita Woolfolk Hoy, and Wayne K. Hoy found in 1998 that teachers' reports of self-efficacy were related to student achievement and motivation. However, research documenting alternatively certified teachers' reports of their own success has yielded mixed results. For example, James Jelmberg found in 1996 that alternatively certified teachers were less confident than their traditionally certified counterparts, a finding that confirmed an earlier study by Frank Lutz and Jerry Hutton. Similarly, Linda Darling-Hammond, Ruth Chung, and Frederick Frelow concluded in 2002 that teachers in New York who had completed traditional preparation felt better prepared in almost all aspects of teaching than those who had not. However, other studies by Edith Guyton and her colleagues as well as John Miller and his colleagues found the groups to be similar.[9]

In a 2007 analysis of the Schools and Staffing Survey, Lora Cohen-Vogel and Thomas M. Smith found no statistically or practically significant differences between alternatively and traditionally certified teachers in how well-prepared they felt. They concluded that alternative certification programs have not substantially changed the pool from which new teachers are drawn and cited further evidence that alternative certification programs do not attract disproportionate numbers of teachers to work in hard-to-staff schools and are not an effective mechanism for eliminating out-of-field teaching.[10]

It is not surprising that research on the quality of alternatively certified teachers is inconclusive since the range of programs and candidates is enormous. Recently, Daniel Humphrey and Marjorie Wechsler conducted an in-depth study of seven alternative certification programs across the nation.[11] Their sample included a range of programs, including Teach For America, which is designed for first-career entrants, North Carolina Teach, which focuses on mid-career entrants from other professions, and Milwaukee's Metropolitan Multicultural Teacher Education Program (MMTEP), which recruits minority candidates who are committed to remaining in the local school system. Humphrey and Wechsler's research documents the many groups of prospective teachers who are targeted by and attracted to alternative certification programs. They conclude in their initial report of findings in 2007 that this enormous variety makes it virtually impossible to generalize responsibly about the candidates, programs, or outcomes of alternative certification.

Because researchers rarely distinguish carefully among different types of programs and groups of candidates, findings from different studies often conflict. As a result, both proponents and opponents of alternative certification programs can find in research the evidence they seek to support their beliefs. Suzanne Wilson, Robert Floden, and Joan Ferrini-Mundy (2001) identify two additional factors that limit the conclusiveness of this body of research. First, it is not possible to determine to what extent such programs' effects are the result of their recruitment and selection policies. Some programs rigorously screen applicants for high-achieving, talented individuals, while others accept anyone who meets minimum standards. Second, based on available research, these authors conclude: "We know nothing about what teacher candidates actually learn in these routes, which seriously limits our understanding of the merits and limitations of such programs."[12]

Data Sources and Methods

We studied participants from thirteen fast-track alternative certification program sites in four states: Connecticut, Massachusetts, California, and Louisiana. All but two of the sites offered most of their training during a five- to seven-week summer program, which provided condensed course work, a clinical component (student teaching or classroom observations in summer school), and some follow-up support during the school year. The programs we studied were operated by a range of organizations, including state departments of education, not-for-profit contractors, universities' departments of education, and school districts.

During the first stage of data collection, we visited the programs and interviewed administrators and faculty about the design and delivery of the program. We interviewed eighty teaching candidates, who represented the range of those in the program, asking why they had chosen an alternative certification program, what they had done in their prior work, what the program provided, and how they assessed their experience. During the second stage of data collection, conducted approximately six to eight months after the new teachers had entered the classroom, we conducted phone interviews with the sixty-five of the original eighty teaching candidates whom we could locate. We asked these new teachers to retrospectively assess their program. Did the program provide sufficient foundation for their early months in the classroom? In what ways did they feel most and least prepared to teach? Did their school support their continuing development? We did not observe classes or examine student performance data, relying instead on the teachers' reports of their effectiveness. These interviews revealed how the teachers, themselves, assessed their training and what they thought might have increased their chances for success in their new role.[13]

FACTORS THAT DETERMINE THE NEW TEACHER'S SENSE OF PREPAREDNESS

Given the variety of programs included in our study, we had expected the participants to report that certain programs were, overall, more effective than others, and we hoped to identify the elements that contributed to the teachers' sense of readiness and confidence during the early months in the classroom. However, it became clear during our analysis that the program is but one factor contributing to the new teacher's sense of preparedness. Also contributing to success are the skills and experiences of individuals who enter the program, as well as the support they receive (or fail to receive) in the schools where they begin their teaching. Humphrey and Wechsler (2007), who conducted their study at the same time, reached very similar conclusions: "We find teacher development in alternative certification to be a function of the interaction between the program as implemented, the school context in which participants are placed, and the participants' backgrounds and previous teaching experiences."[14]

Thus, in assessing the new teacher's sense of readiness for classroom teaching, it would be a mistake to consider only the contribution of the program itself. We must also look back at what these entrants bring to their new career and look forward to see how adequately the school where they begin their career supports them in their continuing development as a teacher. These three elements—the person, the program, and the school—combine to determine the teacher's sense of preparedness during the first year.

Given the variation in candidates, program experiences, and schools as workplaces, success is hard to predict. Notably, these factors are not simply additive, but interact in complicated ways. A candidate with strong subject-matter preparation might succeed despite a weak program if the school he enters offers deep and sustained support. A candidate who lacks solid subject-matter preparation or prior experience with children may fail despite a carefully designed and well-executed program and adequate school-based support. Thus, it is not only unwise, but impossible, to render any summary judgment about alternative certification programs—or even about most individual programs. No program is the sole (or likely even the primary) factor determining a new teacher's success or failure.

The Teaching Candidate's Knowledge, Skills, and Experience

Each participant brings to the alternative certification program a particular background, including knowledge of subject matter and prior work or personal experiences that are relevant to teaching. Who these prospective teachers are, what they know and have done, and what they therefore need or can make use of in their initial training all influence both how individuals experience the alternative certification program and how prepared they will be for their early months of teaching.

Traditional teacher-preparation programs generally are designed for a relatively homogenous group of first-career entrants, who are assumed to bring to their training similar academic course work and only a modicum of relevant life experience. By contrast, the condensed, often minimal, training that most alternative certification programs provide often is justified either on the grounds that prospective teachers who have subject-matter knowledge do not need extensive preparation in pedagogy, or that through life experience these candidates have acquired the knowledge and skills they need to sustain them on the job.

The participants we studied included first-career entrants, mid-career entrants, and current teachers. Some had raised their own children or trained colleagues in other fields, while others had just graduated from college. The amount of recent relevant experience they had in schools differed as well. Some who were already teachers had been in the classroom for years, and some of the mid-career and first-career entrants had volunteered or substituted in schools while others had not.

Knowledge of Subject Matter. Among the candidates interviewed for this study, there were notable differences in how well they knew the subject they planned to teach. Some had completed a master's or doctoral degree in their area of specialization, and others had earned a major or minor in their subject as undergraduates. There were individuals who had routinely used the content of their subject on the job for ten to twenty years. Daniel, a prospective English teacher, had practiced the craft of writing as a journalist. Caleb had current knowledge of the content he would be teaching from his work as an industrial chemist. Others began with little recent knowledge of the subject they once majored in. Nonetheless, these individuals often said they were confident that they had command of the content. As Mark, who had majored in history as an undergraduate said, "Content-wise, I don't have a problem."

Some candidates lacked formal training in their subject but had acquired sufficient knowledge, either on their own or on the job, to pass their state's licensing test. Harold, who had a PhD in chemistry, planned to teach physics or math. Anastasia, with a major in political science, was preparing to teach science. Samantha, who had majored in acting, was a candidate for a license in secondary English. And Regina, a prospective social studies teacher who had majored in criminal justice, read history intensely before the program started. Such individuals brought greater needs to the training programs than did those with strong preparation or recent experience using their subject.

Relevant Experience. Candidates also brought varied experience in teaching-related activities. Some had actually worked as teachers in other settings, such as higher education, outdoor education, or adult classes in English as a Second Language. Manuel, an adjunct college instructor who was seeking a license to teach high school Spanish, had taught for more than thirteen years in higher education. Others had spent extensive time in their prior jobs doing tasks similar to those of teaching—preparing training programs for new workers, teaching formal courses in their content areas, or counseling employees—and they expected that this experience would smooth their transition to classroom teaching. Jane said that as an engineer in research and development she had learned to present complicated information to managers and could foresee doing the same for her students. Similarly, Calvin, who had worked in technology, explained, "My job for many, many years was to take complex technologies and explain them to laypeople. . . . So for me, it's been a form of teaching my whole life, different audiences." Kristin said that, as a result of working for nine years as a lawyer in a district attorney's office, she could think on her feet and was prepared for "whatever could come—different questions [or] a fire alarm." Such individuals generally were undaunted by the prospect of planning curriculum and lessons or translating the content of their subject for students. Many others, however, lacked such experience and confidence.

For most participants, the prospect of engaging with students was not only familiar but very welcome. Many had worked with children and adolescents in various camp and community settings. Mid-career entrants who had raised their own children or worked extensively with youth in sports or religious groups often expressed more confidence than younger entrants about assuming the authority that comes with teaching. In explaining how being a parent prepared her for teaching, a mid-career entrant, Leah, said that a younger novice might see high school students as only slightly older contemporaries, while she regarded her students as "kids," which she thought helped her deal with them more confidently. However, raising children did not necessarily prepare individuals for managing a group of twenty-five to thirty students, some of whom might not share the new teacher's views about the value of formal schooling or expectations about appropriate classroom behavior. As Jane, a mother of several children observed, "The real deal is different."

Candidates' prior experience in schools also varied widely. Some first-career and mid-career entrants were returning to school for the first time since their high school graduation. Although many found the activity and routines of schools familiar and engaging, some were surprised to encounter disorder and disrespect. Anticipating a career change, some candidates had spent time working in schools as volunteers, paraprofessionals, or substitute teachers. Rhoda, a former energy economist, thought that she needed a more realistic experience to supplement the fast-track summer program ahead of her. Intending to become licensed in middle school mathematics, she became a long-term substitute in a seventh-grade math class from January to June. Klara, a first-career Spanish teacher, said that she would have been "very fearful and very frightened" to take on a regular job if she had not had one year in an interim teaching position.

Certain Combinations of Characteristics Led to an Early Sense of Success. Certain combinations of personal characteristics and experiences augured well for individuals' confidence and early sense of success in the classroom. For example, based on these teachers' accounts both before and after they entered the classroom, prospects appeared to be promising for a mid-career entrant who was motivated by the chance for meaningful work and had strong subject-matter preparation, particularly when he or she had used that subject on the job or when earlier work responsibilities were analogous to the tasks of teaching. The candidate's likelihood of success seemed to increase if he or she had raised children, worked extensively with youth, and had become familiar with the current climate and culture of schools by volunteering or working as a substitute.

Ted had completed an undergraduate degree in engineering and a master's degree in materials science. He had directed operations in a technology company, where he supervised fifty-five people. When his company was bought by another and he was laid off, Ted began to act on the career change he had considered for several years. He had been thinking, "Do I really like what I am doing? No, I don't really like what I am doing. If I don't really like what I am doing, why am I doing it?" Despite the pay cut that would come with his career change, Ted's wife encouraged him to consider teaching, which he was drawn to because "it's a public service job, and you can really feel good about your public service." While investigating paths to entry, he taught math for one year in a suburban school district. He explained, "I had my own ideas about how to teach, and I definitely learn by experience, and I learned what ideas worked and what ideas didn't work." However, Ted thought that he had reached the limits of what he might learn on his own: "There were some things that I really, as much as I tried to figure out, had a hard time figuring out." The "biggest was, what makes these kids tick? . . . It's not just figuring out for one kid, it's for the wide range of kids that you get because they are so different." Ted brought to his summer training a very realistic view of the work ahead: "I have had some really hard jobs with high pressure, big pay, and none of them have been nearly as hard as teaching, and anyone considering a career change into teaching has to be prepared to work really hard."

By contrast, a first-career entrant who was ambivalent about teaching, lacked strong subject preparation, or had little experience with youth or familiarity with schools beyond his own education, would be less likely to find the program adequate. At twenty-two,

Chad was entering teaching right out of college. As an undergraduate, he had majored in biology, minored in chemistry, and taken a few education courses, which he thought had been too theoretical to be useful. He was attracted to the practical, condensed nature of the alternative certification program. Because the program was tuition-free, he could earn a license while saving money to buy a house. Not having experienced teaching in other settings or relevant work in other organizations, Chad pursued and landed a job teaching science at his high school alma mater. Once in the classroom, he expressed doubts about teaching long-term, both because his power and influence might be limited in this role, and because he saw teaching as a personal challenge with demands for growth: "It's going to require me to improve myself, especially with social skills. Because I'm a loner, and I don't get out much." Chad said that teaching required him to "think about people," which did not come naturally to him.

Ted and Chad provide distinct contrasts in their readiness for the alternative certification program and for teaching. In fact, few individuals we interviewed entered their program with the full range of qualities and experiences associated with success, although none lacked all of them. Importantly, many candidates began their program with only a few qualifications that might compensate for the brevity of the training and sustain them in challenging work settings. However, the candidates' readiness was only the first factor contributing to their sense of preparedness. The second was what they experienced in the program itself.

The Program that Candidates Experienced

The program contributes to the prospective teacher's development by introducing key topics of education, basic instructional strategies, and an initial opportunity to practice teaching or to observe experienced teachers at work. Typically, programs offered some preparation in generic pedagogy, some attention to subject-specific pedagogy, and some experience in a classroom setting. Although programs often were similar in design, they differed in notable ways, such as the structure of the practicum experiences and the amount of subject-specific pedagogical training. Even within programs, candidates reported having very different opportunities and experiences. Candidates judged certain experiences to be well designed, intense, and useful, but reported that others fell short on several counts.

General Instructional Strategies. Participants rated their program's preparation in generic pedagogy as solid when it included practical skills taught by strong, seasoned teachers. Such course work enabled them to grasp key concepts and strategies relevant to all grades and subjects, such as adapting instruction to students' varied learning styles, planning lessons, and managing classroom behavior. Some candidates said their classes in generic pedagogy were weak. Andrew described his as "abysmal," while Percy called his "ratified common sense." However, others found such training valuable. Regina said that this part of her program was "enormously helpful." Nancy reported, "I learned a ton of things."

Subject-Specific Instructional Strategies. A few programs provided rich sessions in subject-specific pedagogy, preparing the candidates for the particular challenges of teaching individual subjects, e.g., how to initiate discussions of literature in English, how to use manipulatives in mathematics, or how to teach from original sources in history. Although participants said that this part of the program was crucial, programs with scarce resources often did not provide instructors with expertise in each subject for which they offered a license.

In one program, a university instructor taught a methods course for all the program's prospective science teachers, including one in chemistry, one in biology, one in physics, and three in middle school general science. Nancy, a former research biologist who had passed the state teacher's exam in chemistry, general science, and biology, realized that, despite her extensive work as a scientist, she had no idea how to approach her ninth-grade physical science class in the fall. She said she was grateful for this methods course, in which the instructor might announce that the day's lesson would be "an eighth-grade class on convection. And she would run it as a class, and hand us the notes, and we would become eighth graders." Although this approach could never address the particular content needs of all participants who would teach the range of science subjects in middle and high school, everyone could benefit from understanding the process and the "experiment of the day." Occasionally the instructor would stop and step out of role to make observations or answer questions. She also taught topics such as how to assess lab reports or how to ensure safety in the lab, and she showed films of effective and ineffective teaching. Caleb, a chemist, also extolled the value of this class: "It was just wonderful. It was exactly what I had wanted. And here, instead of me having to figure it out, it was being shown to me, how to do it and how to make it a success. . . ." However, both Nancy and Caleb noted that there were only five such sessions during their training, which provided no more than an initial foundation for their work ahead.

Among the candidates we interviewed, there was far more criticism than praise for the subject-specific methods sessions offered by these programs. Sometimes there was simply too little time devoted to this part of teaching to make it useful. For example, during their entire seven weeks of course work, candidates from three sites of a state-sponsored program had minimal subject-specific training (one day of modules to choose from and a few hours of follow-up). Often participants criticized these sessions in subject-specific pedagogy for being poorly planned and taught. Lucy, a prospective social studies teacher who had majored in accounting, said that she was "not much better off" for having participated in the social studies sessions offered by her program. By contrast, mid-career entrant Malcolm, in another state's program, praised his social studies methods course, which was taught daily by experienced social studies teachers.

Clinical Experiences. These fast-track programs typically offered participants student-teaching experiences in summer school classes, under the supervision of cooperating teachers. Participants also expressed widely divergent views of these opportunities, depending largely on the quality of their cooperating teacher. A small number said they worked with exemplary teachers who also served as skillful mentors. Andrew, a prospective chemistry teacher, felt that he and his cooperating teacher were "kindred spirits," and he valued the opportunity to work with him. Such responses were unusual, however. Many other participants harshly criticized their cooperating teachers as "barely competent" or "inexperienced," or they dismissed the clinical component as "next to useless, a waste of money and time." Chad was assigned to a math class even though he planned to teach science. His cooperating teacher occasionally allowed him to take over the class, but offered little feedback. Abraham, assigned to conduct practice sessions for students who had failed the state exam, had no cooperating teacher. At first he was disappointed, but "horror stories" from others in his cohort about the poor quality of cooperating teachers convinced him that, by comparison, his placement was a good one.

Program directors, faculty, and participants believed that doing student teaching in a realistic classroom setting under the supervision of a qualified teacher and skilled mentor could greatly enhance the candidate's sense of preparedness. However, for various reasons, no fast-track summer program we studied offered consistently high-quality student-teaching placements. Many of the problems followed from the fact that summer school, with its short hours, small classes, and selected student body, did not resemble the regular school and seldom attracted first-rate teachers.

Few Programs Received Uniform Praise. Of the programs studied, only one—a small, district-sponsored program that offered training only in special education—elicited uniformly positive comments from participants for being sufficiently focused, substantively grounded, and well supervised. Notably, participants in this program did not do student teaching, but instead observed a small number of exemplary teachers, chosen by district administrators. Candidates in other programs reported more or less satisfaction with their preparation, depending on the match of their individual knowledge, experience, and needs with what their program provided. Some had only praise to offer, saying that the program had met or exceeded their expectations. Usually, however, candidates' judgments were mixed. For example, Leah, who had already taught a year of ninth-grade algebra before enrolling in a state-sponsored fast-track program, said the program had given her a "better angle" on teaching. She had learned how to handle cases of students with special needs, how to address different learning styles, how to conduct parent conferences, and what her responsibilities were as a teacher. However, she "still didn't get better methods for teaching my particular course [mathematics]."

As the prior discussion suggests, the quality of the program proved to be more important to some individuals than others. Several respondents observed that their program was not for everyone, particularly candidates having no recent experience with young people. Taylor said that the program "is going to be what you make of it." It would not work for someone whose attitude was "Tell me everything." Rather, he said, it required someone ready "to seek out opportunities." Some participants came to their program with very measured expectations about what this abbreviated training could deliver, and they emphasized the importance of being "realistic." Jane, a prospective math teacher, said, "I came in with a really open mind. I realize that [the program is] accelerated. I figure, whatever they can give us, let's do it." Dennis, who also planned to teach math, explained that the program gives candidates "a taste" of what teaching will be like, and then it is "up to us to make something of it."

Although most candidates did not expect to be fully trained in a short summer program, some had not realized how little they knew or how much they would need to learn. Theresa, a mid-career entrant, said in July that it was her "mission" to teach, and that she planned to teach until retirement. She thought that her program had "provided excellent training, excellent resources," and looked forward to her second-grade urban class. However, the demands of teaching were much greater than she had expected—"It was bigger than I am"—and she left teaching in October. Similarly, Ruth, a mid-career entrant who said in July, "I feel well prepared," reported the following April that she had found teaching to be much more challenging "in every way" than she had anticipated. She credited the program with providing her "a starting point, a structure" in lesson planning and classroom management, but said that she had to substantially adapt what was presented. She did not feel at all ready to teach a class of low-income students and did not think that she was prepared for the racial issues that emerged in her class-room: "I needed to be taught to deal with black children as a white teacher." In retrospect, she thought that she would have benefited from a longer and more "reality-based," program that allowed her to work under the supervision of a master teacher.

The Schools They Entered

The third factor that influences participants' sense of preparedness is the school site where a new teacher's career actually begins. Although it is obvious that schools differ markedly, it is not always apparent how such differences in the workplace affect a new teacher's opportunity for initial success and continued development. A school that is well equipped, orderly, and focused on learning provides a setting where an individual can continue to grow as a teacher. In such schools, teachers can practice recently acquired skills and develop instructional strategies that make the best use of their personal strengths. Practical and sustained induction, regular feedback about their teaching, and ongoing access to expert teachers' classrooms and advice all contribute to a new teacher's development. However, few schools provide such support, and those that do often are not located in the low-income communities where these candidates are likely to be hired. A school that lacks basic supplies or is riddled with disruption can fail a new teacher who is intent on success. By ignoring the needs of novices, leaving them to flounder without assistance in a sink-or-swim environment, such schools fail these new teachers.

Environments for Teaching. The schools these candidates entered proved to be dramatically different workplaces, either augmenting the new teachers' opportunities for learning and growth or erecting barriers to progress. Some participants described schools that were conducive to good teaching and learning. They had detailed curricula and sufficient supplies to support instruction. They said that their schools emphasized the importance of learning and had strong norms and rules that ensured orderly student behavior and constructive relations with colleagues and parents.

Nancy had hoped to teach in an urban district but could not secure a job before the start of her summer training, and so she agreed to teach ninth-grade physical science in a suburban school. Her new school provided a well-equipped building, a fully developed curriculum, a mentor who taught the same subject, and plentiful resources. With the support of a colleague, she successfully wrote three small grants during her first year to secure science equipment, laptops, and other resources for her department. However, other candidates described schools that were disorderly, lacked basic equipment, had no curricula, provided only outdated textbooks, and left new teachers to fend for themselves.

Even teachers who had solid command of subject matter and thought that their alternative certification program had provided them with sufficient grounding in basic teaching skills, were daunted when they found themselves in schools seemingly set up to discourage good teaching.

For example, Harold, who had a PhD in chemistry, accepted a job teaching physical science at an urban high school four days before the students arrived. He had found the summer program useful and was optimistic about his new career. In summer school, he had taught geometry under the close supervision of a cooperating teacher who provided helpful feedback. Initially, Harold feared that the summer school students might be rowdy and hard to teach, but was surprised to find them engaged. However, his job in the fall proved to be far less manageable. Harold's school provided no induction except for an assigned mentor, who offered no real assistance. He had no classroom of his own and wheeled a cart with all his materials from room to room. He decided not to conduct science experiments because he lacked sufficient equipment and was dismayed by his students' misbehavior and apparent lack of interest. Often students talked back to him and sometimes threw their test papers on the floor when they did not know the answers. By April, Harold reported feeling incompetent and totally overwhelmed by his work.

Teaching Assignments. The character of the new teachers' first assignment proved to be central in determining whether they would succeed during their first months on the job. Individuals who had been hired early and knew what they would teach before the summer training started usually also had assignments that were reasonable—for example, no more than five classes at the secondary level with two preparations in one subject. However, some new teachers—especially those hired very late—taught the courses that were left after more-experienced teachers had been assigned. Typically, these novices had multiple courses to prepare for, sometimes in two subjects or even two schools, and often in the lowest levels of a tracked subject. Sometimes teachers were required to teach part of their schedule outside their field of license, thus dramatically increasing the stress of lesson planning and reducing the chance of success. Although new teachers often encounter such demands, and many leave the classroom because of them, novices prepared in fast-track programs were particularly vulnerable because they had less training and practice to rely on.

For example, Anastasia, an urban high school teacher, was assigned to teach both biology (in which she was seeking certification) and civics (in which she had majored in college). Although she was generally competent in both subjects, preparing to teach two different subjects each day was disheartening. Rebecca, the "one and only" science teacher in a small, urban "second-chance" charter school, was licensed in English but assigned to teach biology, chemistry, physics, and environmental science, none of which came with a curriculum. Samantha, an English teacher in a charter school, had three seventh-grade English classes each day and, over the course of the week, also taught six periods of interdisciplinary classes, one period of speech, and one period of test preparation. When asked what she taught, she responded "Chaos, otherwise known as English."

Not only did a heavy teaching load and large classes make the work of a new teacher especially hard, but it also discouraged the kind of deliberate planning and ongoing reflection that faculty in their preservice program had urged them to continue. In some cases, no amount of commitment to teaching, love of young people, subject-matter knowledge, or just-in-time training could compensate for an unreasonable and unmanageable teaching assignment.

Support from Colleagues. The candidates also described receiving very different levels of support from their colleagues. Some met indifference or hostility from veteran teachers who had nothing but contempt for alternative certification. Others were simply ignored. Harry, a mid-career entrant teaching in an urban middle school, recalled,

> I really felt lost in September when somebody handed me the keys. We had a staff meeting . . . and they said, 'Okay, go work on your rooms,' and everyone else knew what that meant. I walked into my room and had no clue what to do once the door closed behind me.

Julie, an urban first-grade teacher with three years of teaching experience in another country, was generally satisfied with the preparation provided by her preservice program. However, she, too, felt totally unsupported by those in her school. Her assigned mentor never visited her until October (by which time she had already decided to quit), and there was no collaboration among teachers at her grade level. As she explained, "When things were going in a way that I needed help, and knew I needed help, there wasn't anybody to help me out."

In April Chad reported that his assigned mentor—who was in charge of the school's mentoring program—had observed him for only five minutes and answered a few questions. Although he felt that he could get support from other members of his department, he struggled to know what to ask:

I don't really know exactly what I need, and no one actually has the time to listen to my entire story to help me figure out what I need. If I can say, you know, 'Who's in charge of this?' I can get an answer to a question like that. But if I don't even know what I need to know, then I'm lost.

Some other new teachers found a generally congenial spirit in their school, but few offers of help and little in the way of feedback. Given that most participants had, at best, a truncated student-teaching experience, such isolation constrained rather than promoted their further development.

Individuals who experienced more-supportive opportunities to work with colleagues often said that this was the one thing that kept them in teaching. They described having formal coaches or informal mentors who offered materials, lesson plans, encouragement, and advice about how to improve their teaching and how to succeed in the school. Their colleagues became their new teacher educators. Jack, a special education teacher, worked in an inclusion setting with three veteran teachers having ten, sixteen, and thirty-five years of experience. He said that he had "three teachers all year to lean on . . . I don't think I could have made it if . . . I didn't have this group of teachers." Daniel, who taught English in a suburban high school, said that he, too, was very well supported. He conferred daily with his mentor, a veteran English teacher whose classroom adjoined his. He met weekly both with the ninth-grade teachers of other subjects as well as those teaching the same classes he did.

Abraham, a mathematics teacher at an urban high school, also described extensive interactions with colleagues. He met daily with a team of three teachers, including two novices and one veteran. The veteran teacher also served as his mentor. Abraham said that many from his cohort in the alternative certification program complained that they were not getting support in their schools, but he felt that he had plenty. "If there wasn't any support, I think I could have quit. For people who don't have support, I don't know how they do it. But I get a lot—through my mentor, my other teachers. . . ." He described going to peers for advice about how to teach particular topics, such as fractions: "I go to other teachers . . . anybody who will listen . . . I go to a lot of teachers." Stella, a suburban elementary school teacher, also reported that she could go to "all the other teachers" in her school for help. "[I]t's really a good support system."

In the best of school settings such as these, candidates quickly were incorporated into a well-developed, positive professional culture. New teachers had easy and frequent access to teachers at all experience levels, could observe their peers often, and could expect helpful feedback about their teaching. This experience truly extended and expanded learning that began in their preservice program.

Thus, the quality of the school as a place to continue learning to teach significantly influenced teachers' sense of preparedness and success. In some cases, an unsupportive workplace totally undermined any confidence the candidate had gained in his training and discouraged any further learning on the job. In other cases, a school that was well organized for the induction and continued growth of new teachers encouraged a candidate to feel much better prepared and more optimistic about her work as a teacher.

SUMMARY AND IMPLICATIONS

As these examples illustrate, no alternative certification program stands alone in preparing a teacher. Who the candidates are, what training they have had, and what experience they bring greatly influence how instructive and useful the components of the program will be. Participants within the same program have different opportunities, depending on their subject area or their luck in being assigned to a realistic teaching experience or having a skilled and generous cooperating teacher. Finally, the school site can enhance a new teacher's initial experience with ample resources, an orderly environment, a fair and appropriate assignment, and supportive colleagues. Alternatively, it also can thwart growth and early success with inadequate supplies, a chaotic environment, a heavy or poorly matched assignment, and indifferent or hostile colleagues. The person, the program, and the school site all contributed to these candidates' sense of preparedness during their first year and, thus, must be figured into any calculation of the promise of alternative certification programs. This analysis has implications for policymakers, practitioners, and prospective teachers.

Fast-track alternative certification is a deceptively simple idea. In fact, this approach introduces large, often unexpected demands on a program's organizational capacity. Because these programs operated with limited resources in order to keep the costs of training low, they often struggled to provide sufficient preparation. Although the programs we studied opened the profession to some new candidates who otherwise might never teach, they could not effectively serve those who lacked relevant experience, needed practice teaching in typical schools, or had little idea how to teach their subject. Policymakers considering fast-track programs should recognize these demands and fund them adequately. A program that intends to prepare candidates in a number of subjects must employ at least one faculty member who is an expert in each. Good preparation cannot be done on the cheap. When investing in fast-track certification, policymakers should recognize that such programs shift much of the burden of preparing teachers to schools. Thus, they must make a simultaneous investment in beginning teacher induction.

Program directors should recognize the limits of an abbreviated program and concentrate course work on the skills that participants report are most important for getting a solid start in the classroom: basic pedagogy, classroom management, subject-based teaching strategies, and working with students of different backgrounds. For the most part, summer school does not provide a good setting for traditional student teaching, although it may offer an opportunity for candidates to tutor students, observe different teaching styles, and plan lessons. Programs would do well to assess the quality of cooperating teachers in summer schools where they have access and then assign participants strategically. Watching an expert teach may ultimately be worth much more than struggling to teach under the supervision of a weak cooperating teacher. Programs that offer abbreviated preparation to inexperienced candidates would do well to carefully vet the schools in which their candidates will teach. Alternatively, these programs should provide ongoing support and feedback to candidates once they enter the classroom. Such support is difficult for fast-track summer programs to organize, but for teachers who end up in disorganized, unsupportive schools, it may make the difference between staying in the profession and quitting.

School district administrators should recognize that alternatively certified teachers are not fully prepared teachers and will require ongoing support. The fact that a new teacher has received a license does not mean that he or she is well qualified. Consequently, these program participants, like all novices, should not be assigned to the most challenging schools or teaching assignments. Participating in a well-designed induction program and working closely with a skilled partner or mentor will increase the new teacher's chance of success.

Finally, prospective teachers should consider carefully whether alternative certification is right for them. Short programs and practical training are attractive, but may not meet an individual's needs. Having sufficient background in a subject, bringing life and work experience to the classroom, and being ready to learn on the job all increase the likelihood that a fast-track program may be an appropriate pathway into the classroom. However, for individuals who lack any of these, more intensive preservice course work and teaching practice may well be warranted.

This research was made possible by a grant from The William and Flora Hewlett Foundation. However, the views expressed are solely those of the authors.

CHAPTER 5

But Do They Stay?
Addressing Issues of Teacher Retention through Alternative Certification

Jason A. Grissom

One of the key arguments driving the growth and development of alternative routes into teaching is that there are too few teachers coming through traditional teacher-preparation channels to meet persistent growth in schools' demand. Early-entry pathways provide a potential solution by creating new pipelines into the profession for men and women who otherwise would not have chosen to teach. Besides increasing the size of the pool of potential teachers, proponents have argued that alternative programs diversify the pool in terms of ethnic background, work experience, and subject-matter knowledge.[1] Moreover, since teacher shortages are more likely to affect high-poverty schools in urban areas, alternative pathways have the potential to have the greatest impact on the neediest students by channeling new teachers into the most difficult-to-staff environments. Indeed, several studies have found that alternative certification teachers disproportionately work with students who are nonwhite, poor, low-achieving, and urban.[2]

Yet the power of these new programs to address the staffing needs of needy schools is undercut severely if teachers who enter via alternative routes also leave the profession at high rates. Opponents of alternative preparation policies argue that early-entry programs encourage turnover because they require less commitment to teaching and inadequately prepare candidates for the difficulties of the job, which leads to greater stress and lower satisfaction.[3] If alternative certification attracts new teachers who indeed remain in their positions for only a short time, these programs may do little to further the goal of maintaining a stable, robust teacher labor supply. Given the likelihood that high turnover rates contribute to low student performance, alternative certification programs that populate schools with teachers who have high propensities to exit could in fact do more harm to students than good.

In light of these dueling promises and pitfalls of early-entry pathways, this chapter explores the relationship between pathways into teaching and teacher retention. There are two goals: The first is to review and critique the existing research that addresses whether teachers entering through alternative routes leave at higher rates. In general, the results are mixed, with studies finding both positive and negative relationships between alternative pathways and retention, depending on the specifics of the program evaluated. Because of important concerns about the methodological approaches taken by most of these studies, the chapter argues that existing research has left us with a large open question concerning the role of the pathway into teaching in determining how likely a teacher is to turn over.

As a step toward better addressing this open question, the second goal of the chapter is to present findings from a new analysis of nationally representative data from the most recent administra-

tion of the Schools and Staffing Survey (SASS) and Teacher Follow-up Survey (TFS). This analysis illustrates the importance of
considering the kinds of environments in which alternative certification teachers teach in evaluating the relationship between certification type and turnover. The problem arises because schools with
the largest numbers of poor and minority students have the highest turnover rates, irrespective of the certification type of the teachers who teach there. Because alternative programs are a pipeline
for new teachers into the neediest schools, failing to control for
school characteristics may lead researchers to erroneously attribute
a positive relationship between school environment and turnover
to an effect of the pathway instead. The SASS analysis shows that
once school characteristics are included in a multivariate analysis
of turnover decisions, teachers with alternative certifications are
no more likely than teachers with regular certifications to leave the
profession. While this chapter makes no claims about the relative
quality of teachers from alternative pathways, on balance the findings presented here run counter to claims that alternative certification programs hurt the teacher labor supply or harm students by
promoting teacher turnover.

UNTANGLING THE RELATIONSHIP BETWEEN
CERTIFICATION AND RETENTION

As the body of research on teacher labor has grown in recent years,
scholars have cataloged a number of factors that influence teachers' decisions to leave or remain in teaching. Usually these factors
are consistent with a simple opportunity wage theory of teacher
labor markets. As articulated by Guarino, Santibañez, and Daley,
the basic principle underlying much of this literature is that individuals remain in teaching as long as teaching remains the most
attractive occupation available to them.[4] Attractiveness includes

not only monetary compensation but also benefits, good working conditions, and personal satisfaction, among other factors. When the opportunity costs of teaching—that is, the rewards from other work teachers forego in order to teach—in a given position exceed the benefits of continuing to teach, a teacher becomes more likely to leave her school, or even the profession.

Given this framework, it is not surprising that wages are the most studied of factors that influence teacher labor market decisions. Even less surprising, studies find consistently that teachers are less likely to quit or transfer when they are paid more.[5] Yet different kinds of teachers can also respond differently to similar levels of pay, in part because some teachers have more lucrative alternative options than do others. In particular, teachers of exceptional intelligence or ability or who possess especially valuable skills may be able to find much higher-paying work outside of teaching. Consistent with this view, several studies have found that teachers who score highest on college entrance exams or other standardized tests have shorter spells in the profession.[6] For similar reasons, research has shown that teachers who teach in certain fields are more likely to leave than those in others. For example, teachers of math and science, who are more likely to have subject knowledge that holds higher value in the non-teacher labor market, leave teaching at higher rates.[7] Strunk and Robinson find similar results for teachers of foreign languages.[8]

In assessing the impact of alternative certification programs on the likelihood that a teacher stays in teaching, it is imperative that the implications of the opportunity wage theory be considered. For example, teachers who enter teaching via an alternative route may systematically choose schools in districts that offer below-average salaries, or they may be more likely to take jobs teaching science or math. Simple comparisons between alternative- and traditional-pathway teachers in these cases may show that the former leave at higher rates, but it would be inappropriate to conclude that alternative pathways themselves contribute to higher turnover until other factors affecting the teachers' labor market decisions have been taken into account.

Another element that similarly may confound an analysis of pathway into teaching and turnover is the composition of the student body in the school in which the teacher works. Schools with larger minority populations have greater difficulty keeping teachers.[9] Schools with larger proportions of students from poor families face similar challenges.[10] One explanation is that teaching students from minority and poor backgrounds is more challenging, so teachers find such jobs relatively less attractive. Another explanation is that student race and poverty are not themselves determinants of higher rates of turnover but are correlated with other factors, such as lower resource allocations or inadequate facilities that make positions in those schools less appealing. In analyzing the effects of pathway into teaching on turnover, it is important that the researcher is careful not to confuse a teacher's response to the challenges of working in a more difficult environment— namely, looking for a position elsewhere—with a specific effect of alternative certification. Care is especially warranted given that one of the primary rationales for alternative programs is that they funnel teachers into urban schools with large numbers of disadvantaged students.[11]

Unfortunately, prior work that speaks directly to the relationship between alternative pathways and turnover, thin in any case, almost universally fails to account for working conditions or characteristics of alternative certification program participants.[12] Furthermore, Podgursky observes that most studies tend to focus on small samples of teachers in particular alternative programs that may not be representative of alternative programs in general.[13] In some cases, authors report retention rates for alternative-pathway teachers that they label as *high* or *low*, but they fail to show a comparison with traditionally prepared teachers or any other policy-relevant group. In total, the studies in this literature reflect what Guarino et al. call a "lack of rigorous evaluations of alternative credentialing programs."[14]

The results in the existing literature are mixed. Lutz and Hutton study the alternative certification program in the Dallas Independent School District, which admitted 110 "interns" in 1986.[15] Actual retention data are unavailable; instead the authors compare the interns to other first-year teachers with respect to anticipated length of service. They find that 66 percent of the alternatively certified teachers anticipate teaching five or more years, compared to 79 percent of other teachers. Allen also considers alternative certification teachers in Texas, specifically those assigned to minority and economically disadvantaged students.[16] He finds that traditionally certified teachers remained employed at somewhat higher rates but does not include control variables. Darling-Hammond and Berry cite analysis showing that alternative certification program graduates have much higher three-year attrition rates (nearly 70%) than do graduates of four- or five-year training programs (47 and 16%, respectively).[17] Guyton, Fox, and Sisk find traditionally certified teachers to be more positive about their prospects for staying in teaching than alternatively certified teachers in Georgia; however, once again, information on actual retention is not used. None of these studies control for working conditions or teacher characteristics in making comparisons of teachers from different pathways.[18]

Other studies have found teachers entering via alternative certification to compare more favorably to traditional teachers in terms of retention, though these studies continue to suffer from the methodological problems plaguing those whose findings are less encouraging. Kirby, Darling-Hammond, and Hudson draw on data from nine nontraditional teacher recruiting programs that targeted individuals to teach in math and science.[19] Two of these programs, in Houston and South Carolina, are early-entry programs. They find that 96.5 percent of the alternative program graduates were still teaching approximately two years later, the highest retention rate for any of the programs they considered. While they note that this rate is much higher than rates for teachers in general, they also note that their conclusion is based on data from just twenty-nine completers of the two programs. Houston, Marshall, and McDavid show no differences eight years into the careers of a cohort of 131 traditionally and alternatively certified teachers in Houston in terms of satisfaction or intentions to continue in the profession.[20] Natriello and Zumwalt show that elementary teachers from the two pathways had very similar retention rates after three years (85%), and that for English teachers, alternative certification teachers were retained at higher rates (75% vs. 66%).[21] However, they find that 40 percent of alternatively certified math teachers turn over after three years, compared to just 10 to 20 percent of traditionally certified math teachers. Raymond, Fletcher, and Luque examine extensive data on Teach For America (TFA) teachers in Houston from 1996 to 1999.[22] In three out of four years they studied, attrition rates for first-year TFA participants were substantially lower than were the rates for other first-year teachers. Attrition rates following the second year of teaching were much higher for TFA participants than other kinds of teachers, however, reflecting the minimum two-year length of commitment required by TFA. In fact, none of the Houston TFA participants completing their second year in 1998 returned to the system the following year.

One prior study attempts to address the relationship between alternative certification and retention using a national sample. Shen, who compares 13,602 traditionally prepared teachers to 1,119 teachers from alternative pathways using data from the 1993–94 SASS, finds that alternative-pathway teachers were more likely to be undecided about how long they were likely to stay in teaching and were less likely to indicate a willingness to stay in teaching until reaching retirement.[23] He concludes that these teachers are less likely to view teaching as a lifelong career. Unfortunately, Shen does not look directly at whether teachers who entered via alternative pathways in fact left their positions at higher rates. Furthermore, the conclusions of this study have been called into question because of methodological and measurement issues.[24]

One existing study considers pathways and retention while passing the test of controlling for attributes of teachers and work environments. Boyd, Grossman, Lankford, Loeb, and Wyckoff examine comprehensive data from New York City and find that elementary, middle school, and junior high teachers entering the profession through traditional channels have much lower four-year attrition rates (37%) than those entering through Teach For America (85%), the New York City Teaching Fellows program (54%), or temporary licensure (50%).[25] These differences narrow but do not disappear after controlling for differences in the school environments in which the teachers are placed. Because the Boyd et al. results are specific to only two programs in New York, it is unknown whether their findings generalize to programs in other states.

In summary, the literature on the relationship between alternative certification and teacher retention reveals decidedly mixed conclusions.[26] Wilson, Floden, and Ferrini-Mundy suggest that contradictory findings among these studies might be reconciled by the fact that individual programs vary greatly in context, purpose, and requirements across, or even within, states.[27] Such a possibility surely is reasonable. Before we can arrive at the stage of reconciling contradictory results, however, more must be done to separate any effects of pathway from effects attributable to characteristics of program participants or the work environments into which they select.

NEW EVIDENCE ON THE RELATIONSHIP BETWEEN ALTERNATIVE PATHWAYS INTO TEACHING AND TEACHER TURNOVER

As a step toward addressing concerns raised thus far about prior work that has examined the relationship between alternative certification and turnover, this section presents an analysis of the 2003–04 Schools and Staffing Survey (SASS) and 2004–05 Teacher Follow-up Survey (TFS) that takes advantage of the wide set of control variables available in these data. SASS is administered to a nationally representative sample of schools approximately every four years in order to examine teacher demand and shortages, teacher characteristics, and school conditions. Information is collected from district administrators, principals, and teachers, and supplemented with data from the Common Core of Data. In the year subsequent to each SASS administration, survey administrators resample a group of teachers in the TFS. Because one focus of the TFS is the mobility of the teacher workforce, they gather information about teachers' current work status that can be used to analyze turnover between the two survey years.

Note that SASS and TFS employ complex survey design procedures that require the use of appropriate survey data analysis techniques. The analyses that follow utilize necessary survey weights and standard error calculation as outlined in Cox et al.[28] They include only data on the teachers who are present in both the SASS and TFS and who teach in public schools; the analyses below contain information on approximately 4,000 teachers, with sample sizes fluctuating somewhat due to missing data in some specifications.

Identifying Alternative Certification Teachers

Alternative-pathway teachers enter the teaching profession through different programs in different states. Unfortunately, SASS does not ask teachers to categorize their pathway into teaching specifically. Instead, it asks teachers to identify their current certification level. Respondents are given six choices:

1. regular or standard;
2. probationary;
3. provisional;
4. temporary;
5. waiver or emergency; or
6. other.

As defined on the SASS teacher questionnaire, probationary certificates are those issued after the teacher satisfies all regular certification requirements except the completion of the probationary period. Provisional certificates are those issued to teachers "still participating in what the state calls an 'alternative certification program.'" Temporary certificate holders still require additional college course work, student teaching, or passage of a test before regular certification can be obtained. Emergency certification is issued to those with insufficient teacher preparation who must complete a regular certification program in order to continue teaching.

Using a previous iteration of the SASS data, Shen labels any recent recipient of a provisional certificate as an alternative certification teacher.[29] As Ballou points out, however, this strategy alone may lead to misidentification of many alternative certification teachers.[30] In particular, because provisional licenses as defined by SASS are accorded to *current* alternative certification program certificates, it is possible that many program graduates who entered via alternative certification are now holders of regular licenses because they have been recertified by their states. A more complete identification of teachers entering via alternative certification requires the inclusion of both kinds of licensees, not just those who have not yet obtained a regular license.

SASS offers two additional pieces of information that make a more complete rendering of alternative certification holders possible. First, it asks whether teachers hold more than one license in their current state, and, if they hold more than one, they are asked to identify both of them. Thus teachers who had once participated in an alternative certification program and received a provisional license but who had in essence graduated to a regular license are given the opportunity to indicate both licenses on the survey. Second, it asks about the avenues whereby teachers obtained course work on teaching methods and strategies, with one possible answer being *through an alternative certification program.* Former or current alternative certification program participants should identify themselves through this response. In the analysis of teacher retention below, results are presented from two definitions of alternative certification: one that counts any teacher who holds a provisional license as either a first or second license or who responds that she has received instruction through an alternative certification program, and one that ignores certification type and counts only those who respond that they received alternative certification program instruction. The two specifications yield very similar results.

According to extrapolation from the TFS sample, 10.1 percent of all public school teachers are labeled *alternative certification* under the first definition. Approximately 6.8 percent satisfy the second, more restrictive, definition.

WHERE DO ALTERNATIVE CERTIFICATION TEACHERS TEACH?

As argued previously, prior studies of the relationship between alternative certification and teacher retention have failed to consider the implications of alternative certification teachers' selection into schooling environments that are systematically different from those chosen by traditionally certified teachers. Failing to take the characteristics of schools into account could bias one's conclusions if in fact the two kinds of teachers make different selections about where to teach. On the other hand, if the teachers' work environment choices are *not* discernible from one another, one of the principal arguments for alternative certification—that it channels teachers to the neediest students—is called into question.

Table 1 contains information about the characteristics of the schools of the average alternative certification teacher as compared to those of the average regular certification holder who has not participated in an alternative certification program. The alternative certification column includes teachers who meet the first, more expansive definition of alternative certification. Teachers with probationary, temporary, emergency, or other licenses are omitted from the table.

The comparison in table 1 reveals that alternative certification teachers tend to work in very different environments from teachers with traditional certifications. Differences generally are consistent with claims that alternative certification programs specifically benefit traditionally difficult-to-staff schools. Forty-three percent of alternative certification teachers work in urban schools, compared to just 24 percent of regularly certified teachers. Alternative certification teachers are significantly less likely than their regularly certified colleagues to work in suburban (43 vs. 56%) or rural schools (14 vs. 21%). Table 1 also shows that alternative certification teachers work disproportionately in schools with larger percentages of black and Hispanic students and with relatively fewer white students. All of these differences are statistically significant.

On average there are no differences in school Title I eligibility or the fraction of students eligible for free or reduced lunch in the schools of the two types of teachers. However, a closer look at the data shows that this null result is driven mostly by teachers working in suburban schools. Nearly half of the alternative certification teachers working in urban schools are also working in schools in

TABLE 1
*Comparison of Average School Characteristics for Alternatively
Certified and Regularly Certified Teachers, 2003–04*

	Alternative Certification	Regular Certification	t-value for difference	
Locale Type				
Urban	0.43	0.24	4.72	***
Suburban	0.43	0.56	−2.94	***
Rural	0.14	0.21	−2.21	**
Student Race				
Percent Asian students	2.5%	3.3%	−1.27	
Percent black students	23.2%	16.4%	3.01	***
Percent Hispanic students	21.3%	16.2%	1.88	*
Percent white students	51.8%	62.0%	−2.78	***
Student Poverty				
Percent free/reduced-lunch eligible	43.4%	42.6%	0.14	
Title I–eligible school	0.542	0.541	0.29	
School Size and Environment				
School enrollment	920	803	2.5	**
District enrollment	91751	45377	2.07	**
Average pupil-teacher ratio	15.72	16.66	−0.15	
School Type				
Elementary school	0.37	0.49	−3.77	***
Middle school	0.21	0.19	0.92	
High school	0.36	0.27	2.58	**
Charter school	0.02	0.01	3.22	***

*p<0.10, **p<0.05, ***p<0.01

the highest quartile of poverty as measured by free and reduced-price lunch eligibility.

Several other relevant working conditions variables differ between alternatively and regularly certified teachers. While it is natural that working in an urban environment predicts working in larger districts (twice as large as those in which regularly certified teachers work, on average), table 1 shows that they tend to work in *schools* that are on average 15 percent larger as well. This larger school size may be explained by the fact that alternative certification teachers are much more likely than their traditional counterparts to work in high schools and much less likely to work in elementary schools, the latter of which are typically much smaller schooling environments. Middle schools show no significant differences. Alternative certification teachers are also twice as likely to work in charter schools.

In general, these findings confirm those from previous research that alternative certification teachers do tend to work in schools often thought to have the most challenging teaching environments. There does seem to be evidence that alternative certification programs on average help to address the problem of teacher shortages in disadvantaged schools. If graduates of these programs fail to remain in their positions once placed, however, the efficacy of alternative certification as a policy solution is undermined. The next section examines the relationship between alternative certification and turnover more closely.

ALTERNATIVE CERTIFICATION AND TEACHER TURNOVER

For the purposes of examining teacher turnover, it is first helpful to clarify some useful nomenclature. *Turnover* is used to mean any movement by a teacher out of her current position. Turnover can be broken into two kinds: *migration*, which means that a teacher remains in teaching but works in a different school, and *attrition*, which means that the teacher has left the profession altogether. TFS refers to teachers who do not turn over as *stayers*, to teachers who migrate as *movers*, and to teachers who stop teaching as *leavers*. This terminology is adopted here.

It is important to distinguish between attrition and migration from a teacher policy perspective. Reducing attrition is almost certainly a reasonable policy goal because of the capital that teachers build in their first few years of teaching and how that capital translates into student achievement.[31] Because experience is not lost when teachers migrate, whether or not reduction of teacher migration should be a goal of teacher policy becomes less clear. Movement of teachers within the system may be a way of more appropriately matching teachers with schools and students with whom they can more effectively employ their skills, and may thus itself be an important policy tool for school district administrators. On the other hand, if teachers systematically move away from the highest-needs schools, migration may also have costs. In the analyses that follow, these two kinds of turnover are kept distinct.

According to calculations from the TFS, 85 percent of all regular public school teachers continued in the same school between AY 2003–04 and AY 2004–05. Of the remaining 15 percent who turned over, half stayed in the profession but changed schools, while half left teaching altogether, for a one-year attrition rate of about 8 percent. On average, the one-year attrition rate for urban districts was slightly higher, at approximately 10 percent. Of those teachers changing schools, approximately 47 percent moved to another school within the same district. Among teachers with three years' experience or fewer, the probability of leaving teaching between AY 2003–04 and AY 2004–05 was very close to the rate for all teachers, at just over 7 percent. These teachers, however, were more likely to change schools, with 14 percent doing so between the two survey years. Marvel et al. provide a good descriptive analysis of patterns of migration and attrition in the 2004–05 TFS data.[32]

Multivariate Analysis of Certification and Turnover

Do teachers who enter teaching through alternative certification programs turn over at higher rates than teachers with traditional certifications? Using the broader definition of alternative certification, teachers in these programs are less likely to stay in their positions (82.3%) after one year than traditional teachers (85.6%). Though this difference is statistically significant (t = –1.82), it is not especially large. Under the second, narrower definition, the gap is even smaller, 84.4 percent to 85.7 percent, and not statistically significant. Importantly, any difference under the first definition is driven entirely by differences in likelihood of moving, not by the likelihood of leaving; the difference in probability of exiting entirely for the two groups is less than one-half of 1 percent and statistically insignificant (t = –0.33).

To examine these differences with more methodological rigor, a multinomial logit model estimates the probability that a given teacher falls into the stayer, mover, or leaver category in the year of the TFS survey. These probabilities are modeled as a function of a teacher's pathway into teaching, individual characteristics, and the characteristics of her school and district.

Teacher characteristics included in the regression are indicators for whether the teacher is female, black, Hispanic, or the holder of a graduate degree. Age and teaching experience also are included, with experience entered categorically to allow for nonlinearities and to avoid collinearity with the age variable (twelve to twenty years is the omitted category). Recalling the earlier discussion of opportunity wage theory, base salary is included as a control, as is an indicator for whether the teacher holds a degree in mathematics, computer science, or the natural sciences, and an indicator for holding a degree in a foreign language. While some measure of ability would also be preferable to include, such a measure is not readily available in SASS and thus is omitted.

School characteristics included are school enrollment, the fraction of the school that is minority, and the fraction of the student body that is free/reduced-lunch eligible. Indicator variables are used for urban and rural status (suburban is the omitted category), whether a school is an elementary or middle school (high school omitted), and charter status.

Because other studies have limited their comparisons to be between alternative certification and traditional certification teachers, the results shown below compare only those two groups (n = 4,043). An alternative specification that used data on all TFS teachers but created a third category of "other certificates" gives virtually identical results for the relevant variables.

Table 2 shows the results using the broader definition of alternative certification. In estimating a multinomial logit model, one of the categories of the dependent variable must be selected as the base category against which the other categories are compared. In table 2, *staying* is the base category. *Leaving* is shown in the four columns on the left, and *moving* is shown in the four columns on the right. The model is estimated four times to inspect whether one's inference about the relationship between alternative certification and turnover may change when controls for teacher and working environment characteristics are or are not included.

Coefficients are represented as relative risk ratios. Relative risk ratios can be interpreted as the relative change in likelihood of falling into the given category relative to the base category, given a 1-unit change in the independent variable in question. Values greater than 1 indicate increasing likelihood, and values less than 1 indicate decreasing likelihood. Thus, for example, we might inter-

TABLE 2

Multinomial Logit Prediction of the Probability a Teacher Leaves, Moves, or Stays after One Year Using Broad Definition of Alternative Certification (Provisional License or Alt Cert Courses)

	(I)	(II)	Leavers (III)	(IV)	(V)	(VI)	Movers (VII)	(VIII)
Alternative Cert.	1.100	0.921	1.039	0.881	1.472**	1.303	0.954	0.856
	(0.201)	(0.189)	(0.209)	(0.197)	(0.224)	(0.241)	(0.172)	(0.176)
School Characteristics								
School size (100s)		0.994		0.992		0.999		1.007
		(0.014)		(0.014)		(0.012)		(0.013)
Fraction minority		1.006*		1.005		1.006**		1.005*
		(0.003)		(0.004)		(0.002)		(0.003)
Fraction free/reduced-lunch		0.996		0.996		1.003		1.004
		(0.005)		(0.004)		(0.004)		(0.004)
Urban school		1.543*		1.511*		1.432**		1.440**
		(0.343)		(0.371)		(0.236)		(0.247)
Rural school		1.053		1.259		1.150		1.152
		(0.213)		(0.290)		(0.179)		(0.184)
Elementary school		1.130		1.025		1.152		1.156
		(0.200)		(0.207)		(0.162)		(0.188)
Middle school		0.926		0.903		1.553**		1.691**
		(0.214)		(0.218)		(0.328)		(0.368)
Charter school		1.117		1.093		1.272		1.025
		(0.288)		(0.330)		(0.386)		(0.343)

*Teacher Characteristics**

Female	1.225	1.164		0.947	0.896
	(0.161)	(0.194)		(0.111)	(0.135)
Black	1.431	1.226		1.274	0.858
	(0.441)	(0.439)		(0.210)	(0.182)
Hispanic	1.200	1.094		0.986	0.790
	(0.390)	(0.384)		(0.296)	(0.287)
Has MA	0.941	1.001		1.018	1.165
	(0.160)	(0.191)		(0.154)	(0.184)
Age	1.031***	1.032**		0.985	0.982*
	(0.011)	(0.013)		(0.009)	(0.010)
Degree in math, computer science, or natural sciences	0.889	0.907		0.784	0.829
Degree in foreign language	0.834	0.984		1.049	1.234
	(0.268)	(0.340)		(0.342)	(0.479)
Base salary (in $1,000s)	1.013*	1.015*		0.989	0.984*
	(0.007)	(0.008)		(0.007)	(0.008)
N	4576	4043	4576	4043	4576	4043

*p<0.10, **p<0.05, ***p<0.01. Coefficients expressed as relative risk ratios. Controls for years teaching (1, 2 or 3, 4 or 5, 6 to 8, 9 to 11, 21 or more) also included in models II, IV, VII and VIII.

147

pret a relative risk ratio of 1.028 on the *age* variable in column III as indicating that for each year older a teacher becomes, the relative risk of being a leaver rather than a stayer would increase by a factor of 1.027, other factors held constant. Conversely, the relative risk ratio of 0.980 on the same variable in column VII implies that the probability that a teacher becomes a mover rather than a stayer decreases as she ages. In other words, as teachers grow older, they become less likely to change schools and more likely to leave the profession altogether as they move closer to retirement.

Before considering the results, note that an alternative logit model that does not break turnover into migration and attrition but looks only at *turnover or not* and controls for no other factors would yield an odds ratio on alternative certification of 1.28 (t = 1.89), which is significant at the 0.10-level (not tabulated). This odds ratio implies that holding an alternative certification increases the odds that a teacher does not remain in her same position from one year to the next by about 28 percent. Such a result, consistent with several descriptive studies that have found substantially higher turnover rates for alternative certification teachers, would not appear to support alternative certification as a policy solution to the problem of teacher shortages. However, the results in columns I and V, which similarly show the simple bivariate comparison of alternative and traditional certification teachers, only with turnover broken into attrition and migration, show that this increased likelihood of turning over is not driven by exit behavior. The relative risk in column I is not significantly different from 1. Instead, turnover among alternative certification teachers is driven by movement within the profession: Teachers with alternative certifications are much more likely than teachers with traditional certifications to change teaching positions. As noted earlier, the policy implications of turnover due to migration rather than turnover due to attrition potentially are quite different.

A main theme of this chapter is the contention that inclusion of characteristics of teachers' work environments is a necessary step in untangling the relationship between alternative certification and retention that previous studies have ignored. Columns II and VI in table 2 show why. When school characteristics are included in the estimation, the relative risk ratio on alternative certification for leavers actually falls below 1, though it is not statistically significant. The magnitude of the relative risk ratio for alternative certification for movers also falls precipitously, and while remaining above 1 can no longer be distinguished from 1 statistically.

The relative risk ratios on some of the other variables in columns II and VI illustrate why inclusion of these characteristics is important. In particular, the ratios on *minority enrollment* and *urban school* are statistically greater than 1 in both columns. Teachers in minority and urban schools are more likely both to transfer and leave the profession. As table 1 showed, teachers who entered teaching via alternative certification disproportionately locate in these schools. Not only is this selection effect an important driver of the correlation between alternative certification and turnover in these data, but, in fact, accounting for this selection also makes the correlation undetectable in a statistical sense.

Columns III and VII exclude school characteristics but instead control for teachers' observable characteristics. Showing these results separately from the results including only school characteristics is important because they represent a different type of selection: selection of different kinds of participants into alternative certification programs rather than those participants' selection into their work environments. Again, the relative risk ratio is statistically indistinguishable from 1 in both columns, implying no underlying difference between alternative and traditional license holders in likelihood of turning over. Congruent with previous research, age and teaching experience are significant predictors of turnover behavior.[33] Contrary to predictions of opportunity wage theory, however, these data find no evidence that holding degrees in mathematics, computer science, natural sciences, or foreign languages affects teacher attrition or migration. Surprisingly, they also show some evidence that teachers are more likely to leave teaching when their base salaries are higher, though caution should be exercised in drawing a strong conclusion from this result because of the potential endogeneity of teacher-pay and quit decisions. Note that excluding this variable from the regressions has no impact on the estimate of the alternative certification coefficient.

Columns IV and VIII show the results of the estimation with both school and teacher characteristics included. With all controls included in the regression equation, the relative risk ratios for both leaving and moving for alternative certification teachers fall below 1 and remain statistically insignificant. Holding other relevant factors constant, table 2 offers no evidence that teachers entering the profession via alternative routes are more likely than traditional teachers to turn over.

Perhaps owing to the relative recency with which alternative certification programs have become widespread, the average alternative certification teacher has only 7.8 years of experience, compared to an average of 15.5 years for traditional teachers. One worry that arises is that these experience differences make direct comparison between the two groups unreasonable, even after controlling for experience levels. As a check, alternative models were run first interacting alternative certification with experience categories and then limiting the sample to teachers with five years of experience or less, each with full sets of control variables.

In the first case, the main effect of alternative certification on both leaving and moving was statistically indistinguishable from a null effect. None of the interactions for leavers were statistically significant, and the interactions of alternative certification and holding one or two to three years of experience were both smaller than 1, implying that, if anything, novice teachers are more likely to stay put if they entered teaching via alternative certification than if they entered via a traditional pathway. In the second case, the relative risk ratio on alternative certification was 1.44 for leavers and 0.63 for movers, though neither value was distinguishable from a null coefficient of 1.

To address the possibility that the null result for alternative certification is due to a misclassification of many traditional teachers as alternative certification teachers because of the expansiveness of a definition that includes all provisional license holders, the main analyses were re-run using the narrower categorization that included only those teachers who reported having received instruction on teaching methods and strategies through an alternative certification program. The results are summarized in table 3. The magnitude of the relative risk ratios for alternative certification across all four specifications are nearly identical to the results shown in table 2. As in table 2, the relative risk ratios for alternative certification in columns IV and VIII are both smaller than 1 and statistically insignificant. Again, no evidence of an important relationship between alternative certification and turnover is uncovered.

CONCLUSIONS

Prior studies that have included analysis of turnover rates among teachers entering the profession via alternative pathways have suffered from two deficiencies. The first is narrowness of scope. By limiting inquiry to one cohort, one program, or one state, researchers have been unable to come to consistent conclusions about the relationship between pathway and retention or to generalize about those conclusions beyond the specific population under study. The second deficiency is a failure to consider selection into pathways

TABLE 3

Multinomial Logit Prediction of the Probability a Teacher Leaves, Moves, or Stays after One Year Using Narrow Definition of Alternative Certification (Alt Cert Courses Only)

| | Leavers | | | | Movers | | | |
	(I)	(II)	(III)	(IV)	(V)	(VI)	(VII)	(VIII)
Alternative certification teacher	1.042	0.839	0.974	0.816	1.286	1.142	0.866	0.778
	(0.219)	(0.199)	(0.237)	(0.223)	(0.283)	(0.291)	(0.200)	(0.211)
School characteristics?	no	yes	no	yes	no	yes	no	yes
Teacher characteristics?	no	no	yes	yes	no	no	yes	yes
N	4178	3701	4178	3701	4178	3701	4178	3701

*p<0.10, **p<0.05, ***p<0.01
Coefficients expressed as relative risk ratios.

152

and work environments and instead to focus only on unadjusted turnover rates as evidence of the efficacy of alternative pathways as a policy solution. As prior studies have shown and this chapter reiterates, working conditions are especially important to include in any analysis in this area because of the purposefulness with which alternative preparation programs have been aimed at providing teachers to the hardest-to-staff schools. Indeed, analysis of the SASS/TFS data shows that teachers holding alternative certifications work disproportionately with minority students in urban environments. Hence, failing to consider that the peculiar challenges of working in such schools makes *any* teacher more likely to look for work elsewhere, regardless of her route of entry into teaching, may lead one to assume an effect of certification on turnover where there is only an effect of working conditions.

The analysis presented in the second half of this chapter, designed to address both kinds of deficiencies, suggest that drawing erroneous conclusions from simple descriptive analysis is a real danger. While teachers holding alternative certifications are more likely than regularly certified teachers to turn over—though this turnover is mostly due to movement to other teaching positions—evidence of a relationship disappears once school and teacher characteristics are included in a regression. A reasonable conclusion that can be drawn from this result is that teachers who enter the field through an alternative certification program on average *are* less likely to stay in their positions from year to year, but that this lower likelihood appears to be due largely to characteristics of the schools in which these teachers work and not to attributes of the alternative certification programs that helped them get there. Claims that alternative certification programs encourage turnover by insufficiently preparing teachers to handle the difficulties of the profession do not find much support.

While there is a real need for the use of national data in this literature, the SASS/TFS analysis undertaken here comes with two important caveats concerning potential measurement issues with these data. First, the surveys do not neatly group teachers into categories based on their pathways into teaching, and while steps have been taken to use information beyond simple certification type to separate them into groups, misclassification of teachers is an important concern because of the potential for bias. Second, there is some question about the accuracy with which the TFS reports the work status of participating teachers.[34] Attenuation of the coefficient on alternative certification because of misclassification or misreporting for both of these variables could be important drivers for this chapter's central null result, a possibility that other analyses should explore.

A criticism that has been leveled at other studies that have used the SASS/TFS data to examine the effects of alternative certification programs is that the data do not permit the researcher to distinguish among preparation programs that can have wildly different goals and methods.[35] That criticism applies here as well. The use of these data trades off the ability to characterize what kinds of alternative certification programs are more successful at promoting teacher retention than others for the opportunity to say what the retention effects of alternative certification programs are *on average.*

Some alternative preparation programs no doubt are better than others at producing teachers who stay in the profession. This variation likely explains the range of results of prior research studies that have looked at the retention of teachers from particular locations or programs. Identifying especially successful alternative certification programs and their characteristics across different contexts using multistate, multi-cohort data would be a significant contribution to the current research base.

These results also point to the need for additional work on the question of whether alternative certification programs train teachers who are of similar levels of effectiveness as those trained in more-traditional teacher-preparation programs. The literature on this point is explored further in chapter 6. If alternative certification teachers are as able to manage classrooms, structure lessons, and deliver content, a strong case might be made for increased investment in alternative pathways into teaching, particularly if further analysis using other data sets corroborates the finding that alternative certification programs do not promote turnover. On the other hand, if the quality of instruction delivered by alternative certification teachers is significantly lower, then there is an important equity implication. Alternative certification would be systematically channeling ineffective teachers into classrooms with the most disadvantaged students. The fact that those teachers likely would be staying in their jobs would be of small consolation.

Assessing the Effectiveness of Teachers from Different Pathways: Issues and Results

Marsha Ing and Susanna Loeb

Teachers enter the classroom through a range of pathways, which vary in their amount and focus of course work, their required experiences in classrooms, their recruitment and selection criteria, and their costs. While many teachers still obtain their certification through completing a four-year undergraduate program or a one- or two-year master's program, others enter through a variety of other pathways, including early-entry programs with very little course work on teaching or supervised experiences in classrooms prior to teaching. Information on the effectiveness of teachers from different pathways can help to improve state policies governing preparation requirements, the design of preparation programs, and school and district teacher-selection and -placement policies. Yet, until recently, research examining the relationship between teacher preparation and teacher effectiveness was quite limited. This chapter summarizes the relatively new research on this topic, highlighting factors to consider when estimating effectiveness. It concludes that early-entry programs have shown positive effects for some subject areas and grade levels and provides useful information about how better to structure preservice preparation requirements and practices.

Teacher effectiveness is multidimensional. Teachers can be effective at improving the learning of students in one area of the curriculum or another; they can be effective at promoting student self-esteem, motivation, or engagement. Measuring teacher effectiveness is a complex task. Ideally, we would like to see how students progress across various dimensions during the time they are exposed to a particular teacher. However, in practice we rarely have measures of student progress in any one of these dimensions over time; and, even when such measures are available, it is difficult to distinguish the contribution of a teacher from other factors such as home life, peers, and school climate, all of which also affect student progress. Understanding the effectiveness of specific teacher pathways is also quite challenging. If teachers from each pathway were randomly distributed across and within schools, then we would not have to worry about these other factors when assessing the differential contribution of teachers from each pathway; but, they are not. Some pathways lead teachers to certain types of schools and students while other pathways lead to other types of schools and students. As such, assessments of the effectiveness of pathways to teaching are best viewed according to the dimension of effectiveness they address, the extent to which they accurately capture a more-complete measure of effectiveness, and the extent to which they convincingly distinguish teacher pathway effects from other factors contributing to student progress.

This chapter focuses on measures of teacher effectiveness derived from student performance gains on standardized tests. As discussed further below, there are drawbacks to this approach. An alternative would be to analyze how pathways into teaching affect teacher behaviors, such as instructional practices and career decisions, instead of student outcomes. One benefit of this approach is that it eliminates the need to match teachers to the students they teach. Of course, it does have the disadvantage of not actually measuring student progress; the link between teacher behaviors and students is established separately. A second alternative would be to study student progress on measures other than test performance. Unfortunately, the research in this area is sparse.

Even when analyzing only student test performance, accurate estimation of pathway effects is complicated. A naive estimation would compare average student performance of teachers from one pathway into teaching with average student performance of teachers from another pathway into teaching. The temptation then arises to conclude that one pathway to teaching is more effective than another because it has a greater average student performance. Such a conclusion would be premature because, as discussed above, teachers are not randomly assigned to classrooms. Because of systematic sorting, any reliable analysis will need to separate the effect of specific pathways from other factors affecting students, including home environment and school climate outside of the classroom.

Clear definitions of the pathways are also important. Often teachers' preparation experiences within the same pathway differ dramatically, while, at the same time, there is substantial overlap in teachers' preparation experiences across pathways. How pathways differ can vary by grade and by subject-area specialization. It is difficult to derive implications for reforms if we do not understand the substance and details of different pathways. In addition, there is selection of teachers into pathways. Some pathways, for example, attract teachers with particularly strong academic skills. Separating the true benefit of the pathway experiences from pathway recruitment and selection differences can help to clarify the implications for reform decisions.

The results of research on teacher pathway effects are mixed. There is some evidence to suggest that there are positive effects from particular early-entry programs, especially in math; other studies find little difference in teacher effectiveness across pathways. In what follows, this chapter articulates the importance of clearly defining pathways and then discusses the potential limitations of using students' standardized test performance as a measure of the value added by teachers. It then summarizes research on student achievement for teachers from different pathways, discusses measurement and methodological issues that might account for differences in the literature, and provides suggestions for future research on teacher pathways.

DEFINING PATHWAYS

One difficulty in assessing the effects of pathways on student learning comes simply from the difficulty in distinguishing among pathways.[1] Categorizations such as *traditional* or *alternative* rarely capture consistent differences in teacher experiences across pathways.[2] "Alternative" programs can range from fifth-year master's degrees to one-year internships to highly selective six-week summer programs to nonselective summer programs. "Traditional" pathways can range from undergraduate programs to fifth-year programs to master's programs. Humphrey and Wechsler found dramatic variability in structure and content across seven programs that were all considered "alternative."[3] As an example, preservice field-based experience ranged from few opportunities during the summer for New York City Teaching Fellows to yearlong opportunities for those in the Teacher Education Institute program in California. If we see that one pathway produces teachers who, on average, are more effective than teachers from another pathway, we will have difficulty knowing how to use that information unless pathways are clearly defined.

Similarly, loosely defined pathways often overlap. Some programs that are typically classified as alternative share many experiences and requirements with programs that are typically classified as traditional. For example, some early-entry programs are closely affiliated with institutions of higher education that also run more-traditional teacher-education programs (see programs in Baltimore and New York City).[4] These institutes often aid in designing and teaching the course work for the early-entry programs, and, as a result, the course work can be quite similar to that used in their traditional programs. This overlap is important to consider when interpreting the results of studies that estimate differences across pathways. If a study finds no differences across pathways, the result could be driven by the minimal differences in experiences or other characteristics, not necessarily by the lack of an effect of particular program features, were these features to actually vary.

Given the variability within and the overlap across loosely defined pathways, research showing average differences in teacher effectiveness across pathways may tell us little about productive directions for policies and practices. We learn more from research that carefully defines pathways so that they differ as cleanly as possible in their characteristics. With these definitions, we can learn more about the effectiveness of different approaches as they relate to the recruitment, selection, and development of teachers.

Just as the pathways must be clearly defined to make results meaningful and useful, the measured effects must also be clearly categorized. One pathway or program may have a positive effect on increasing ninth-grade standardized math scores. Another may have an effect on diminishing the achievement gap among fourth graders in reading. Some pathways are more likely to be effective at preparing teachers for particular grade levels or subject areas than others; and some pathways are likely to be more effective with certain types of students. Most studies of teachers' value-added to student achievement to date have used data on student performance in math and reading. Most, though not all, have also used data on students in elementary or middle schools. To the extent that programs or pathways excel at preparing teachers for other areas of teaching, these studies may not fully capture differences. These potential differences in effectiveness by area can help us to reconcile seemingly conflicting results in the research literature and point us in directions for future research.

LIMITATIONS OF STUDENT TEST PERFORMANCE MEASURES

Student learning is a logical metric with which to measure the effectiveness of teaching.[5] However, available measures of student achievement are never perfect indicators of what students know or what teachers have taught. Researchers have raised general concerns about whether these tests are valid measures of the domains of knowledge that we care about, whether they reliably measure student learning, and, even if they do, whether they reliably measure the aspects of learning that teachers affect.[6]

Our schools' goals for student learning span a range of areas: math and reading; science and history; music; art and athletics. Within each subject area there are many dimensions or domains. In math, for example, students can encounter number theory, fractions, algebra, and geometry, among other topics. English language arts includes decoding, reading comprehension, and writing. No single test or sequence of tests could cover all the material even within a single subject area in a single grade. Standards and curricular frameworks help to bound the possible scope of the material, but not nearly enough for tests to cover the full curriculum.

As such, in choosing or developing tests there are always trade-offs. Some knowledge and skills are easier to assess through standardized tests than others, and often we choose to sacrifice more difficult-to-measure elements for those that are easier. Whether these trade-offs are important enough to invalidate the tests as measures of student knowledge in the chosen domains is up for debate. It is important, however, to know what the tests do and do not measure so that this information can be used in drawing conclusions about the implications of any finding.

Part of understanding the validity of a test is knowing both the ease with which the test results can be manipulated through small changes in practice and the incentives for teachers to change their practice in order to manipulate test results. For example, if there are high stakes for teachers attached to the tests, then there will be incentives for teachers to do what they can to increase test scores. While ideally this would be through improving learning, there may be easier routes, such as cheating or teaching test-taking practices that do not improve students' knowledge in the domain nor benefit them in the long run, but may raise test scores in the short run.

Even if the tests do validly measure the domains of interest, they may not be good for measuring student learning over time. We are often not only concerned with student status at a particular point in time but also in the amount of learning or change that occurs as a result of instructional experiences. To measure student change over time requires following the performance of the same student on several occasions. In most cases, this means comparing student performance in one year with performance in subsequent years. Lissitz and Huynh point out that a major assumption of using changes in test performance is that the content across grade levels is comparable.[7] For example, we might measure student math performance in one grade level and then again in another grade level. The assumption is that test items at these different grade levels accurately measure knowledge of math and are not confounded with other skills, such as reading. If the linguistic complexity of math items at the later grades interfered with a student's ability to demonstrate their knowledge of math, there are multiple dimensions being measured. This multidimensionality makes it difficult to tease out whether student performance is actually reflecting knowledge of a single dimension (math) or a result of multiple dimensions (math and reading).

Finally, for the tests to be useful for estimating the effects of teachers, they must not only validly measure change in knowledge over time, but they must also measure those aspects of change that could be affected by teachers. Some changes in knowledge or ability may be more a function of developmental change than of classroom learning. If the tests were to primarily reflect these aspects of learning then they would not be valid instruments for measuring teacher effects. Some researchers have argued that the tendency for studies of program and teacher effects to find greater effects in mathematics than in English language arts in elementary schools reflects this phenomenon, because learning in math is more influenced by experiences in school, while progress in learning to read is relatively more influenced by factors outside of school.[8] The degree to which the measures are aligned with and influenced by the curriculum and instructional activities affects the validity of the test as a measure of a teacher's value-added to student learning.[9] The timing of testing programs may also affect the ability of research to isolate teacher effects. For example, if achievement tests are given early in the year, how much of the gain between the prior and current years should be attributed to the student's current teacher and how much to the teacher in the previous year?

In addition to concerns about the external validity of the test measure, poor reliability of the test may also hamper its usefulness for assessing teacher and teacher-pathway effects. Even the domains and topics specifically selected for the tests will be measured with error. This is a particular concern at the tails of the performance distribution, for the students who score either quite high or quite low. Most standardized tests aim to distinguish among students, and because many students tend to have approximately average knowledge, most tests include more questions that measure knowledge at approximately the average level. Fewer questions aim at the lower and upper levels of knowledge and, thus, there is more measurement error at these tails. Computer-adaptive tests can efficiently target questions to all levels, but most research on teacher effects to date has not used these tests. Measurement error becomes an even greater concern when we look at changes over time because the error on each test is compounded. Often we are particularly concerned with the effects of practices and policies on the lowest-scoring students, and these are just the ones for whom the test is least accurate.

In sum, tests are imperfect measures of student learning, even in the domains that they cover. A single outcome measure or set of measures will never reflect the range and dimensions of student knowledge.[10] Tests also vary in the accuracy with which they reflect true ability in a specific domain.[11] These difficulties are compounded when we look at changes over time and link them to teachers and try to adjust for differences in the schools and classrooms in which these teachers teach. Shulman summarized these concerns on the use of student outcome measures by saying that

> . . . indeed, as if the standardized tests were not sufficiently questionable as sufficient reflections of achievement, the analyses of change, replete with corrections for initial differences and measurement unreliability, as well as the needed premises about equal impact of teachers across all students, are seriously deficient.[12]

Despite these limitations, test scores *do* have their advantages. We are unlikely ever to have a perfect measure of student learning.

While we could forsake trying to link teachers to student learning as a result of this inherent imperfection, in doing so we are likely to lose information that could be helpful for improving practices if used thoughtfully. We do know that traditional measures of success such as teacher satisfaction and feelings of preparedness are fraught with error, and we have not yet developed accurate instruments for capturing high-quality instruction. The imperfections of the test measures should be considered when drawing implications from the research, noting which domains of learning they cover and which they do not, and assessing the extent to which the particular test used is likely to have been subject to gaming behaviors linked to high-stakes accountability. With these caveats, however, these outcome measures provide some of the only information we have on the effectiveness of different pathways into teaching and of education policies and practices, more generally.

METHODS TO ATTRIBUTE OBSERVED DIFFERENCES IN STUDENT ACHIEVEMENT TO TEACHERS

Even with clear definitions of pathways and valid and reliable measures of student achievement, researchers must design their analyses carefully in order to avoid attributing to teachers and to their pathways what are actually the effects of other factors. Teachers from some pathways teach in schools and classrooms with characteristics that are systematically different from those of teachers from other pathways. For example, in New York City, new teachers from the largest early-entry program, the Teaching Fellows, on average, taught 42 percent black students, 50 percent Hispanic students, and 89 percent students eligible for free lunch, compared with teachers from the traditional college-recommended route who taught 34 percent black students, 39 percent Hispanic students, and 76 percent free lunch–eligible students. If those differences affect student learning, then the researcher must account for them in order for their estimates of effects not to be biased. There are several approaches to making this adjustment, and these approaches vary in their advantages and disadvantages.

Random Assignment

Random assignment of teachers to classrooms is the cleanest approach for addressing potential differences in the teaching context. Mathematica Policy Research, Inc. conducted such a study of pathways into teaching, randomly assigning students to Teach For America (TFA) teachers and non-TFA teachers.[13] The goal of randomly assigning students to teachers or teachers to classrooms is to create equivalent groups of students through chance assignments.[14] While the researcher is able to observe some student traits, there are always important characteristics that the researchers cannot observe, such as students' enthusiasm for learning. Random assignment of adequately large numbers of teachers and students can create equivalent contexts along dimensions that include both observable and unobservable characteristics.

The main drawback of random assignment is that it is both costly and difficult to implement. The random assignment of students to particular teachers is not always feasible and successful implementation is always of great concern.[15] As an example, students and their parents may work against random assignment, trying to get into particular classrooms with particular teachers. Because of the cost of implementation, the scope of the studies is often small and not representative of the full population of interest. Campbell and Stanley describe randomization as "not for the purpose of securing representativeness for some larger population" but "solely for the purpose of equating experimental and control groups or the several treatment groups."[16]

Statistical Controls and the Value-Added Methodology

Most studies of the effects of pathways into teaching are not able to implement large-scale random-assignment designs and instead rely on available data, usually administrative data from school districts or states. The researchers then use statistical adjustments to account for differences in the context of teaching across teachers from different pathways. *Value-added modeling* is a general classification used to describe regression-based approaches to estimating the effects of teachers or teacher characteristics on growth in student achievement.[17] McCaffrey, Koretz, Lockwood, and Hamilton describe value-added models as "any educational achievement model that uses gain scores or regresses current scores on prior scores."[18] The models differ in terms of how they define value-added, the data they need, and the assumptions that they make.

Most models attempt to control for aspects that influence student achievement, such as students' prior achievement or the demographics of the student population at the school.[19] The motivation for including these controls is to attempt to limit factors that might explain student achievement so that the model can more accurately attribute changes in student achievement to the instructional opportunities provided by a particular teacher. For example, if teachers from one pathway systematically taught students with lower initial achievement than teachers from another pathway, if we then looked at student achievement at the end of the year without adjusting for initial achievement, we might attribute lower scores to teachers from the first pathway even if the learning was actually equal or even greater.

Value-added studies of teacher effects differ along a number of dimensions. Some studies use student achievement as the outcome measure and control for prior achievement while others model student learning as the change in test scores directly. Some include characteristics of students such as their gender, age, or race, while others include indicator variables (or fixed effects) for each student, and by doing this, control for all time-invariant characteristics of students, even those not observed. Some include classroom characteristic measures such as the average prior test scores of students, while other studies do not. Some include school characteristics while others include indicator variables for schools, thus estimating the effects of pathways by comparing teachers within the same school. There is no consensus in the research community as yet concerning which model is optimal. Many studies try multiple specifications in order to test the robustness of their findings. That said, all reasonable studies attempt to adjust for likely differences between teachers from different pathways in the characteristics (both measured and unmeasured) of the schools and classrooms in which they work.

TEACHER PATHWAY EFFECTS

There are two potential mechanisms through which routes into teaching can produce effective teachers. First, through recruitment and selection, they can attract individuals who will be good teachers, irrespective of the teaching education they receive. Second, they can provide opportunities for individuals to develop their teaching skills through course work and fieldwork in classrooms. The effect of any program or route into teaching is a combination of these two mechanisms. Traditional university-based teacher-education programs have tended to focus on the second mechanism, with little emphasis on recruitment and selection. Alternative routes vary more in their emphases. The TFA program, as an example, is highly selective. It received approximately 19,000 applications for the 2006 academic year for approximately 2,400 spots. The applicant pool included 10 percent of the senior class at Spellman and Yale and 8 percent of the senior class from the California Institute of Technology.[20]

The effect of teachers from a given pathway is a combination, then, of both selection and opportunities to learn. Few studies to date have done a good job of separating these two mechanisms, though such separation would be useful for aiding the design of more-effective routes. If programs are successful solely through selection or recruitment, then the key to improving teaching would be to understand which selection criteria are important (for example, it could be exceptional performance on some measure of ability) and then work to attract individuals with these selected characteristics. The resources currently expended on preparation could instead be used to increase the appeal of teaching for individuals with the characteristics identified as important for successful teaching. If on the other hand, the mechanism through which a pathway is effective relies on the educational opportunities it provides, then understanding what those opportunities are and providing them to other potential teachers could be the most productive approach to improving teaching. In practice it is likely to be a combination of these two mechanisms that determine whether programs are effective.

As noted above, both alternative routes and the traditional routes to which they are compared can vary a great deal, and, as a result, the research results on the effectiveness of alternative routes relative to other routes into teaching is mixed. Much of the extant research has compared teachers from the TFA program to other teachers in their schools. TFA is a national program that recruits recent college graduates for teaching in schools that districts have had a difficult time staffing. The program requires a two-year commitment from its participants and provides a five-week summer preparation institute prior to teaching, as well as supports during teaching. The studies of TFA, as summarized below, have tended to find some positive effects of TFA teachers in math performance and little effect or negative effects in English language arts (ELA).

Studies that estimate the effects of teachers from other early-entry programs tend not to be as positive.

Decker, Mayer, and Glazerman from Mathematica Policy Research Inc. conducted a study of TFA teachers that randomly assigned teachers to students in an attempt to equate the teaching context of TFA and non-TFA teachers.[21] They found positive effects on elementary math achievement for TFA teachers compared to teachers who did not participate in TFA. These effects held true across grade levels, geographic locations, and subgroups of students. This study did not include information about the preparation experiences of the teachers who were not trained by TFA, and thus the precise nature of the comparison is not clear.

Raymond, Fletcher, and Luque found similar results to the Decker et al. study using data on elementary school teachers from a Texas school district.[22] Although this was not a random-assignment study, the researchers did control for student characteristics (ethnicity, free or reduced-lunch eligibility, and prior achievement), teacher's years of experience, classroom characteristics (free or reduced-lunch eligibility and prior achievement) and school characteristics (ethnicity and free or reduced-lunch eligibility). They found that over the course of a year, the students of TFA teachers gained more on tests of mathematics (but not reading) relative to students of other teachers.[23] The authors also found less variability in the student performance of TFA teachers compared to the other teachers, although the group of other teachers came from a diverse set of routes and the study did not separate the comparison group by route. In a study using data from the same district, Darling-Hammond, Holtzman, Gatlin, and Heilig separate TFA teachers who have gained certification from those that have not and find more positive effects for the certified teachers.[24] Uncertified teachers, both those from TFA and those from other programs, do not show as strong value-added as certified teachers in this study.

A third set of studies used data on third- through eighth-grade teachers in New York City schools. Both Kane, Rockoff, and Staiger and Boyd, Grossman, Lankford, Loeb, and Wyckoff used a variety of specifications, controlling for multiple student, classroom, and school characteristics, and including indicator variables for schools and/or students in order to adjust for differences in teaching context between TFA teachers and other teachers.[25] The two studies used slightly different comparison groups. The Kane et al. study compared TFA teachers to teachers who obtained certification through recommendations from their teacher-education program or who obtained certification through a process of individual evaluation from the state. The Boyd et al. study compared TFA teachers to just the college-recommended teachers. In both cases, the studies found that the students of TFA teachers, on average, experienced greater gains in achievement in math and less in reading than students of other teachers. The Boyd et al. study separated students in upper elementary school (fourth and fifth grade) from those in middle school (sixth through eighth grade) and found that the positive effect of TFA teachers on student performance in math was specific to the middle school, though the negative effect in reading held for both elementary and middle school students.

Only one study to our knowledge has examined the value-added of teachers from different pathways to high school students' test-score performance. This lack of research is due largely to data limitations. High school students are taught by multiple teachers each year, and often the students do not take standardized tests in each year—or if they do, the tests are broad enough that it is difficult to link them to particular teachers. North Carolina, however, does require end-of-course exams for high school students. Using this information, Xu, Hannaway, and Taylor find that students of TFA teachers learn substantially more during the course of the year than students of teachers from traditional routes.[26] They estimate that the difference in effectiveness between the routes is approximately equal to twice the difference between the average first-year and average second-year teachers. There is not a large enough sample size of TFA teachers in North Carolina high schools to separate the effects by subject area and the results are an average of teachers in algebra I, algebra II, biology, chemistry, geometry, physics, physical science, and English I. The positive results for TFA teachers are driven largely by positive effects in math and science classes. The models include student indicators and thus identify the effects of the pathways by comparing changes in individual students' learning over the time they spent with teachers from different pathways.

In summary, there is some evidence that TFA teachers are at least as effective as other teachers in their schools at improving the math achievement of students. Their effectiveness appears greater at the middle and high school level than in elementary school. At the elementary level, there is evidence that they are not as effective as teachers from more-traditional university-based programs at teaching English language arts. Of course, one of the reasons TFA teachers are in schools is because those schools have trouble recruiting teachers from traditional university-based programs. Zeichner and Conklin question these conclusions about the effectiveness of TFA teachers; they argue that the research does not adequately describe how the TFA teachers were prepared or how their preparation differs from that of non-TFA teachers. They conclude that based on "the lack of information about the characteristics of the teachers, one cannot differentiate the effects of teacher characteristics from those of teacher education programs."[27] As Zeichner and Conklin suggest, these results do not necessarily indicate that TFA provides prospective teachers with uniquely effective preparation opportunities; in fact, the positive TFA effects may largely be due to their emphasis on recruitment or selection rather than preparation per se. Nonetheless, as mentioned above, the combination of selection and preparation characterizes any route into teaching, and thus these results are as accurate an assessment of the effectiveness of the route available today.

While much of the research effort has focused on evaluating the relative effectiveness of TFA, there are many other alternative routes and even early-entry specific routes which offer diverse training opportunities and serve substantial numbers of prospective teachers. For example, in the 2004 school year, TFA provided 360 new teachers to New York City schools, while the New York City Teaching Fellows, a different early-entry program, provided 2,441 new teachers. Teaching Fellows is modeled on TFA in that it places substantial emphasis on recruitment and selection and provides opportunities to learn about teaching during a relatively short preparation period, often in the summer.[28] It is not quite as selective as TFA, and its preparation opportunities differ. As an example, while TFA requires its prospective teachers to coteach in a classroom during the summer program, Teaching Fellows are more likely to observe in the classroom of a New York City public school teacher for their field experiences, with more limited opportunities for independent teaching.[29]

Boyd, Grossman, Lankford, Loeb, and Wyckoff and Kane, Rockoff, and Staiger also evaluated the effectiveness of Teaching Fellows teachers. The results are somewhat similar though not as positive as those for TFA.[30] Boyd, Grossman, Lankford, Loeb, and Wyckoff found that relative to the students of traditional-route teachers, the students of first-year Teaching Fellows do not improve as much in their performance on standardized tests in English language arts (ELA) in either elementary or middle school, and do not improve as much in their performance in math in elementary school. The negative effect in ELA is approximately the size of the difference in effectiveness between the average first-year teacher and the average second-year teacher in the sample. There is no discernible difference between students of teachers from these routes in middle school math. After the first year, however, Teaching Fellows do, on average, as well as teachers from college-recommending programs, except in middle school ELA. As Kane, Rockoff, and Staiger point out, while the difference between the Fellows and traditional or college-recommended teachers is evident in the first year, the variation in effectiveness as measured by the teachers' value-added to student achievement varies much more within programs and pathways than between programs and pathways. That is, there are both very good and very poor teachers in all of the routes studied.

As might be expected, the effect of pathway appears to be larger for first-year teachers than for other teachers. Because of this, the total effect of the pathway on teaching quality in a district is a combination of the number of teachers the pathway provides and the experience of those teachers. Boyd, Grossman, Lankford, Loeb, and Wyckoff reasoned that "if one pathway consistently has higher turnover, even if its teachers do well relative to those in other pathways with the same experience, the pathway may not, on average, be providing the most effective teachers."[31]

To investigate this further, the authors simulated the effects of pathways accounting for different tendencies for teachers from different pathways to leave New York City teaching jobs. They found that for middle school math, students from Teaching Fellows and TFA teachers perform higher than students with teachers from other pathways regardless of how long the pathways have been operating. For elementary math and ELA, the simulation results indicated that when the pathways are just introduced in a district, students with Teaching Fellows and TFA teachers initially gain less in their test performance than students with teachers from other pathways; but, within a couple of years there is little difference across pathways. ELA middle school students from Teaching Fellows or TFA teachers tend to have a lower performance during the first year of program operation but outperform other students by the fifth year of program operation. The results suggest that overall differences in the effectiveness of teachers across pathways are not large, once variation in attrition is accounted for, although there are meaningful differences in the effectiveness of first-year teachers.

In a smaller-scale study of student learning, Miller, McKenna, and McKenna examined the relative effectiveness of teachers from a university-initiated early-entry pathway in Georgia.[32] According to the researchers, this program was not highly selective, unlike the TFA and the Teaching Fellows programs. Entry requirements did not include test performance or a minimum grade point average. The program included course work over the summer that complied with Georgia Certification Standards. During their first year of teaching, students received mentoring from university faculty and public school teachers and enrolled in additional course work. The researchers created matched pairs of alternative and traditionally certified teachers who started teaching in the same year, taught the same subjects, at the same grade level, at the same school. They compared classroom performance of fifth- and sixth-grade students on reading and math assessments; the researchers did not include any covariates in their analyses because they concluded that there were no differences between the groups of students in terms of a pretest measure. The authors looked specifically at teachers with three years of teaching experience and found no difference on student performance in reading and math between the two groups of students. These results are consistent with the other available studies that find discernible effects are largest in the first year. Even if there were initial differences, these might be gone by the third year. In addition, this study was so small, including only eighteen classrooms, that it may not have been able to distinguish effects even if those effects were meaningfully large.

Studies that compare the effects of certified teachers to noncertified teachers do not provide direct evidence of differences between alternative- and traditional-route teachers because both of these routes lead to certification, but they do provide some information of whether and, if so, how routes into teaching can produce teachers who are differentially effective. Most teachers in the United States are certified. For instance, in 1999–2000, 94.4 percent of public elementary and secondary teachers were certified in their main teaching assignment. In theory, certification keeps individuals who are likely to be poor teachers out of the classroom. The evidence on the effect of certification is, however, mixed.

Recent studies in New York City and North Carolina found that students of certified teachers learned more, on average, than did students of uncertified teachers, though a similar study in Florida found no difference.[33] The studies in New York and North Carolina found that teachers who passed their certification exam (the Liberal Arts and Science Test in New York and the Praxis II in North Carolina) showed higher student achievement in math. For example, teachers who passed the Praxis II produce on average student achievement gains that were in the range of 3 to 6 percent of a standard deviation higher (in math) than those who failed.[34] Comparing the effect of this gain to that produced by experience, the study found that the average teacher who failed the test, were he/she allowed to teach regardless, would likely produce the same level of math achievement in his/her second or third year of teaching as a novice teacher who passed the test.[35] The study also shows how test cutoff criteria can generate a number of false negatives (individuals who fail to pass the test but might have been high-quality teachers) and false positives (individuals who make the cutoff might turn out to be poor teachers), calling into question the signal value of certification tests.[36] Also worrying is evidence that raising cutoff scores might reduce the supply and racial/ethnic diversity of the prospective teacher pool.[37]

Another line of research that sheds light on the effects of different routes into teaching estimates the effects of features of preparation programs on teachers' value-added to student learning. While research in this area is new, one study in New York City finds that teachers who have opportunities to practice skills that are well connected to the work in the classroom have greater value-added in their first year of teaching. For example, programs that oversee student-teaching experiences more carefully or require a capstone project supply significantly more-effective first-year teachers. Teachers who have had the opportunity in their preparation to engage with student work (listening to a child read aloud for the purpose of assessment, planning a guided reading lesson, or analyzing student math work) also show greater student gains during their first year of teaching, as do teachers who have had the opportunity to review curriculum.[38] While this work is still in its infancy, it suggests that the learning opportunities that potential teachers have during their preparation can affect their value-added to students, at least in their first year of teaching.

In summary, the research literature to date linking teacher pathways into teaching with student achievement gains is sparse. Almost all existing studies have assessed the effects of one program, albeit a large one, TFA. The results here have been mixed, with indications of positive effects of TFA teachers, particularly in math, and some indication of negative effects in elementary reading. The size of the positive effects in math range from small to relatively large, up to twice the difference between the average first- and second-year teachers at the secondary level. The estimated effects for other routes, such as the New York City Teaching Fellows, are somewhat less positive, though consistent in that the elementary reading effectiveness appears the least strong and the math effectiveness for older students, the most strong. The variation in teacher effectiveness across teachers that went through the same pathways is larger than the average differences in teacher effectiveness between pathways. These differences, particularly the negative effects of Teaching Fellows, are often stronger in the first year of teaching than in subsequent years. Overall, the research is not rich enough to provide clear policy directions; however, it does point to the potential benefit of bringing in teachers with strong content knowledge and academic ability in the high school, while at the same time suggesting the potential importance of other types of knowledge—perhaps pedagogical knowledge for teaching reading or knowledge of child development—particularly in the elementary school.

OTHER MEASURES OF TEACHER EFFECTS

Student test scores are not the only measure of student progress worth considering in an analysis of teachers from different pathways. Other student outcome measures such as course-taking behaviors, motivation, high school graduation, or post–high school plans can provide further information on effectiveness. Unfortunately, there are few studies that use these alternative measures for students.

In their study of TFA teachers, Decker et al. did include non-achievement student outcomes, such as whether students were retained at grade level, attended summer school, were tardy or chronically absent, or were well behaved, in addition to student achievement outcomes.[39] Using data from teacher reports of student behavior and school and district records and the random-assignment methodology, they find no evidence that students in TFA classrooms were more likely to be retained at grade level or attend summer school compared to students in other classrooms. There was also no difference between TFA and other teachers in school-reported absenteeism or disciplinary incidents (suspensions, expulsions). Teacher reports of absenteeism and disciplinary incidents showed some differences in student behaviors, with TFA teachers reporting higher levels of problems with physical conflict among students and greater interruptions during class to deal with student disruptions compared to non-TFA teachers.

Other studies have used measures of teacher quality not directly linked to student outcomes. For example, Miller, McKenna, and McKenna use measures of instructional practice based on observations of their sample teachers. They find no evidence of a difference between the teachers from the early-entry route and other teachers in their Georgia sample in either lesson components or pupil-teacher interactions.[40] A new study of alternative-route teachers in New Jersey uses interviews with superintendents and principals to assess the quality of instruction provided by alternative-route teachers.[41] It finds that these administrators are satisfied with the performance of alternative-route teachers, especially in high schools where they cite the importance of their subject-matter competency. In keeping with the test-score literature, the superintendents and principals are less positive about the effectiveness of the alternative-route teachers in elementary school, citing the importance of understanding child development. In a related study, Jelmberg surveyed principals on the instructional skills and instructional planning of traditionally certified teachers and alternatively certified teachers in New Hampshire.[42] While his response rates were low, calling into question the generalizability of the results, he found that principals rated traditional-route teachers higher than teachers from the New Hampshire alternative routes on both instructional planning and instructional skill.

Teaching quality is multidimensional and there are multiple measures of quality worth exploring in studies of teachers who entered through alternative routes; however, the extant research has only limited analysis of differences across teachers based on pathways using anything other than student performance on standardized tests. Existing research does show little difference between groups, though the differences that are there are consistent with the test-score-based research.

IMPLICATIONS FOR RESEARCH

The research to date on the effectiveness of different pathways into teaching is sparse, but there are a number of high-quality studies that shed light, not only on the effectiveness of specific programs, but also on the factors to consider when evaluating the effectiveness of different pathways into teaching more generally.

First, as many have pointed out, not all alternative or early-entry pathways are the same. Programs differ dramatically in their recruitment and selectivity and also in the opportunities for learning they provide.[43] If we see a positive effect of early-entry teachers in one analysis and not in another, it may well be because the early-entry programs are quite different in the two analyses. Similarly, the comparison group, whether it comprises traditional-pathway teachers or a mixed group of teachers from "other" pathways, can vary significantly as well. Differences across studies could stem from these variations in the comparison group even if alternative-pathway teachers enter through similar routes.

Second, the relative effectiveness of teachers from different pathways can vary depending on the grade, subject area, and school characteristics of the teaching context. The research suggests, for example, that teachers from highly selective early-entry pathways are more effective in math than in reading, and more effective in upper grades than in lower grades. Even if a particular pathway appears less effective in both math and ELA, that pathway might actually focus on other areas, such as teaching special education students whose learning is less likely to be accurately measured by the standardized exams. Understanding the programs targeted subject area is important for assessing its effectiveness. Similarly, most early-entry programs serve urban schools that have been historically difficult to staff, and thus, most of the evidence on the relative effectiveness of alternative-route teachers is specific to these types of schools. These results may not generalize to other schools.

Third, differences in effectiveness between early-entry teachers and teachers who have completed a traditional teacher-education program can differ by years of experience. As an example, studies in New York City indicate that the relatively poor performance of early-entry teachers primarily takes place during the first year of teaching. These findings imply that not only will the research be more informative if it clearly distinguishes effects by years of experience, but also that the total benefit of a pathway is likely a combination of the estimated effectiveness of its teachers and their attrition rate. If one pathway is particularly good starting in the second year, but very few of its teachers stay past the first year, then its total contribution will be far less positive than if its teachers have a greater tendency to stay beyond the first two years of teaching.

Fourth, our ability to accurately measure the effectiveness of teachers from different pathways depends on the measures of student progress that are available. Often we do not have—and it is costly to collect—reliable measures of student learning or of teaching. There are clearly many domains of learning, and we may not be able to capture the ones in which we are interested. For example, we rarely have measures of achievement gains in high school classes. Some measures may also be less sensitive to teaching quality.[44] A measure used in one study might be highly related to the types of instructional opportunities provided to the students and might be highly sensitive to the effects of instruction, while a measure used in another study might reflect the national goals or standards that are less related to the instructional opportunities of a particular classroom. Attention to the types of measures used in these studies might help account for differences in conclusions about the effects of teachers from different pathways.

Finally, research on different pathways includes different data sources and methodological approaches. The research is clear that teachers from different pathways teach systematically different students and in systematically different schools. All reasonable studies of the effectiveness of pathways into teaching work to adjust for these differences in teaching context. Studies with random-assignment designs or those with very large sample sizes and detailed data on students are best able to make these adjustments. The results of empirical studies are more or less believable to the extent that they are convincingly able to make these adjustments. Did the random assignment work to equalize baseline characteristics of students and schools across pathways? Did the analysis compare teachers within schools or do a convincing job of controlling for differences across schools?

Aggregating research findings across studies requires consideration of each of these factors. What are the characteristics of the pathways in question and of the students in question? What are the subject areas covered and the experience levels of the teachers? How is student progress measured, and how are differences in teaching context accounted for? To date the research is not rich enough to paint a full picture of the relative benefits of different pathways along multiple dimensions of subject areas, grade level, student characteristics, and teacher experience. However, the research currently available demonstrates that keeping these distinctions in mind is important; further research will contribute to our understanding largely to the extent that it can provide insights into this variation in effectiveness.

CONCLUSIONS

Recent years have seen the emergence of a range of pathways into teaching. While many teachers still enter through traditional undergraduate programs, others enter through graduate programs or through selective or nonselective early-entry programs with five or six weeks of course work and limited classroom experiences before beginning as a full-time teacher. The development of new routes into teaching has occurred largely in the absence of information concerning which aspects of preparation are particularly important for new teachers or which characteristics and skills of individuals are particularly important for teaching. It is just this type of information that will be useful for improving the programs that we have and for developing new policies and practices for entering teachers.

The research to date shows that the alternative/traditional pathway dichotomy is not particularly useful for learning about entry pathways because there is so much variation across both alternative and traditional programs, and because there is often substantial overlap between the two groups as well. Instead, the research is more useful when it identifies the differences between specific programs and practices.

As described above, there are two potential mechanisms through which routes into teaching can produce effective teachers. They can, through recruitment and selection, attract individuals who will be good teachers. Alternatively, they can provide opportunities for individuals to develop their teaching skills through course work and supervised practice in classrooms. The effect of any program or route into teaching is a combination of these two mechanisms. Traditional university-based teacher-education programs have tended to focus on the second mechanism, with little emphasis on recruitment and selection. Alternative routes vary more in their emphases, and some have put substantial effort into recruitment and selection.

The available research does not paint a complete picture of either optimal recruiting and selection criteria nor optimal preparation opportunities; however, for a relatively small group of studies, they do provide useful and consistent results. In particular, highly selective early-entry pathways, such as TFA, appear to provide teachers for difficult-to-staff schools who are as effective, or more effective, than other new teachers in their schools at improving the achievement of students, particularly in math and at the middle and high school level. These early-entry pathway teachers have been less successful at the elementary level and in English language arts. Less selective early-entry routes may not be as effective, though the information on their value-added to student learning is very limited. On the whole, the research suggests the importance of balancing strong recruitment and targeted selection—both of which have been overlooked by most traditional teacher-education programs—with useful opportunities to learn about teaching through course work and through supervised experiences in classrooms.

Taking Stock:
Future Directions
for Practice and Research

Pam Grossman and Susanna Loeb

In taking stock of the existing evidence about alternative routes, what can we conclude? First, diverse routes into teaching are not new; historically, much of teacher education was a local endeavor, with school districts growing their own teachers. Both district programs and normal schools recruited teachers from the local area and focused squarely on the school curriculum teachers would actually be teaching. In this sense, such teacher preparation represented an early form of the locally grounded programs that school districts are currently running, included the Boston Residency Program and the New York City Teaching Fellows.

While the diversity of pathways into teaching is not new, recent years have seen a dramatic increase in the numbers of teachers who are entering schools, particularly schools serving many low-income and low-achieving students, through alternative certification programs. For example, in the 1999–2000 school year in New York City, none of the 7,539 new teachers entered city schools through early-entry alternative routes. In the 2003–2004 school year, 2,800 of the 7,782 new teachers came through these alternative routes.[1]

We also learn that alternative routes have been successful in attracting a new pool of teachers into the classroom, although the characteristics of this pool differ by program. Highly selective programs like Teach For America and the New York City Teaching Fellows have been successful in attracting prospective teachers with much stronger academic qualifications than those who enter teaching through more-traditional pathways. As an example, while many districts have had a difficult time recruiting enough math and science teachers with strong content knowledge to staff their middle and high school classes, Teach For America received applications from 8 percent of the senior class from the California Institute of Technology.[2] However, not all alternative routes are highly selective, or select based on the prior academic achievement of prospective teachers. For example, some alternative routes target paraprofessionals while others aim to increase the diversity of the teaching workforce. This variation in teacher characteristics by program illustrates the difficulty of making sweeping generalizations about alternative certification programs.

While many of the debates about the merits of alternative certification have compared the new programs to traditional, university-based teacher preparation, alternative-pathway teachers generally are not replacing teachers from more-traditional certification programs. Rather, they have tended to replace teachers with emergency credentials or temporary licenses or to fill vacancies that resulted from an increase in the number of teachers demanded by districts or schools, due, for example, to class-size reduction or increases in retirements. As an example, during the period between 2000–2004, when the number of teachers in New York City entering from alternative certification grew from essentially none to over 2,800 new teachers, the number of new teachers from traditional programs only dropped by 426 (from 2,618 to 2,192) teachers, while the number of emergency-certified teachers dropped by 3,279 (from 3,886 to 607) teachers.[3]

The introduction of highly selective alternative routes has meaningfully changed the characteristics of teachers who serve students in traditionally difficult-to-staff schools. For example, the introduction of the alternative routes in New York City described above led to a 28 percent drop in the number of all teachers in the poorest 10 percent of schools who had failed their general knowledge certification exam and a 24-point increase in the average SAT score of these teachers. There is some evidence that such changes in teacher qualifications improve student test performance, at least in mathematics. They do this by replacing some of the teachers that are likely to be the least effective. However, teacher qualifications, even impressive qualifications like high GPAs from highly selective colleges, are not the same as teaching quality—the quality of actual instruction.

We know less about the instructional quality of teachers who enter teaching through different pathways. As the chapters in this volume indicate, the evidence on how teachers from alternative routes perform in classrooms is mixed. The existing evidence for Teach For America indicates that its teachers are more effective in math than in English language arts, and more effective in middle and high school than at elementary grades.[4] The evidence on other early-entry alternative routes into teaching is both sparser and less positive. Moreover, there is far greater variation in the achievement gains of students, as measured by value-added methodologies, across teachers who entered teaching through the same pathway than there is variation in the average effectiveness of teachers across pathways. This variation suggests that the existence of alternative routes into teaching, even highly selective alternative routes, alone cannot ensure high-quality instruction, particularly in high-poverty schools.

We argue that part of a solution to the problem of teaching quality may lie in taking the best innovations of alternative routes, particularly with regard to recruitment and selection of a talented and diverse pool of candidates, and marrying that with stronger preparation and support for new teachers during their first year on the job. It may also be the case that a diversity of routes into teaching is a good thing for schools and for students. Teachers with strong content knowledge bring some skills into schools, while teachers with strong roots in the community or understanding of child development may bring others. Optimal routes into teaching may differ in important ways for different pools of teachers. Yet, in order to design effective routes we must do a better job of learning from routes that are already operating. What is working, what is not, and for whom?

The simple dichotomy between alternative and traditional programs does not capture the significant differences in characteristics across routes. In this concluding chapter, we suggest a different way of thinking about categorization of certification programs and suggest directions for future research and practice in this area.

REFINING OUR TERMS

Rather than using the broad and increasingly meaningless designations of *traditional* and *alternative* to categorize programs, we suggest a different kind of typology that distinguishes programs based on the nature of the provider, the focus of recruitment and selection, the labor market needs being addressed, and the timing and focus of preservice preparation, which would include both course work and field experiences.[5]

Who Is the Provider?

Who provides preparation is one of the primary factors that distinguish among programs. In the current market, three types of providers dominate teacher preparation: colleges and universities, private providers, and districts—although in a few cases, states run their own teacher-preparation programs as well. Colleges and universities provide the vast majority of traditional preparation programs either through undergraduate or master's programs. In addition, colleges and universities provide much of the course work for many alternative programs and even run some early-entry programs of their own.[6]

Independent organizations also run alternative-preparation programs. Teach For America is a prime example; not only do they do their own recruitment and selection, but they also run their own preservice preparation in the summer prior to entry into the classroom. Even TFA, however, partners with institutions of higher education (IHEs) to fulfill course-work requirements. Perhaps in response to difficulties in filling vacancies, some large urban districts also run their own alternative routes, such as the Boston Teacher Residency (BTR) program.[7] While BTR aims to increase the diversity of Boston teachers, other district-run programs aim to fill shortage areas, such as special education and middle and high school math and science. Often districts partner with nonprofits and with IHEs to run their programs. The New York City Teaching Fellows, for example, is a partnership between the New York City Department of Education and The New Teacher Project, an independent nonprofit which provides support for recruitment and designs and delivers portions of the preservice program to Teaching Fellows.[8] At the same time, local universities provide the formal course work and supervision. We might call these mixed models.

Focus of Recruitment Efforts

Alternative certification programs also differ in their recruitment practices. Recruitment matters, in large part because the larger the pool of prospective candidates, the more selective a program can be. Some programs focus their recruitment efforts on graduates of elite colleges and universities and are highly selective, while others are much less selective. Some programs recruit exclusively from specific populations—former military, Peace Corps volunteers, or paraprofessionals within a local district—while others recruit broadly. Some programs recruit locally, while others advertise nationally. Targeted and aggressive recruitment is also a relatively new phenomenon. More-traditional university-based preparation programs rarely have actively recruited or focused on purposeful selection. The recent introduction of programs that put great effort into recruitment through advertising campaigns and visits to highly selective colleges has demonstrated the potential power of such recruitment endeavors. We know less about what attributes programs might select for to ensure highly effective teachers; leadership, resiliency, content knowledge, general knowledge, experience working with students, and charisma are all possible selection criteria.

What Labor Market Needs Are Addressed?

Programs differ as well in their efforts to address specific needs of state or district labor markets. Some programs focus exclusively on high-needs certification areas, such as special education, secondary math and science, or teaching English-language learners. Such programs are more narrowly focused on producing sufficient numbers of high-quality teachers in targeted areas. The Teaching Opportunity Program, an early-entry program run by the City University of New York, for example, focuses exclusively on teachers in a few key areas: secondary math, secondary science, and Spanish.[9]

Other programs recruit more broadly, hoping to attract teachers across a range of subject areas and grade levels. Such programs may be more interested in broadening the pool of prospective teachers than meeting specific labor market needs. Until recently, traditional programs have tended not to target particular subject areas or grade levels, instead offering a wide array of certification programs. At the other extreme, as might be expected, district-run programs are often the most responsive to district needs.

Timing and Focus of Preparation and Ongoing Support

The most significant difference between alternative and more traditional programs of teacher education resides in the timing and focus of preservice preparation. In their purest form, traditional programs provide all of the course work and field experience requirements prior to a teacher's entry into the classroom as a teacher of record, while early-entry alternative routes provide only a small part of the requirements prior to entry. In actual fact, these features vary widely among alternative certification programs. As others have noted, in this volume and elsewhere, alternative-route programs include those with minimal preservice preparation, consisting of a six-week summer experience, as well as programs that require a full year of coteaching prior to assuming full responsibility for a classroom. While some programs require only minimal course work, other programs include significant course-work requirements, which in some cases mirror the requirements for more-traditional programs. Even traditional routes vary substantially in the timing and content of course work and field experiences. As an example, a recent survey of New York City teachers found that approximately one-fourth of students in traditional teacher-education programs were fulfilling at least part of their student-teaching requirement on their own as a full-time classroom teacher, a pathway characteristic that usually defines alternative routes.[10]

In order to refine our distinctions among alternative-route programs, we could distinguish between programs that frontload preservice preparation into the first summer and give participants full responsibility for a classroom in the fall—what we've termed *early-entry* or *fast-track programs*, and those that provide eased entry into teaching with ongoing course work and clinical experience throughout the first year of teaching—what are now being called *residency models*. These two broad types differ significantly in the amount of support and opportunities to learn about teaching they provide to novices.

Even within each of these models, the nature of course work, field experience, and mentoring can vary tremendously.[11] Some programs tailor the summer preservice course work to the particular needs of early-entry teachers, focusing on classroom management and local curricula for teaching core subjects, while others focus broadly on the purposes of education in a democracy, or principles of learning. Within early-entry programs, the fieldwork requirements can vary as well, from models that require participants to essentially coteach a summer course, as Teach For America does, to those that require primarily classroom observations and minimal responsibility for teaching. Finally, while most alternative certification programs require some form of mentoring or support during the first year, the nature of that support can vary tremendously, both in terms of what programs intend and what participants experience, as the chapters in this volume make clear.

Given the great variation among alternative routes, defining them as a single group masks important variations and limits our ability to understand and improve these pathways. A typology built upon a combination of features would allow for more precise description, as well as more accurate comparisons among programs. Here we are proposing the four dimensions described above:

1. the nature of the provider;
2. the focus of recruitment and selection;
3. the labor market needs being addressed; and
4. the timing and focus of course work and fieldwork preparation.

Such a typology could distinguish among the newly emerging residency programs, such as the Boston Teacher Residency program and the Chicago Residency program, which provide extensive field experience—a full year of coteaching in the classroom of an experienced teacher—prior to certification, from programs that require only a few weeks of summer school teaching. The Boston Teacher Residency program is run primarily by the district, with the support of local universities, and targets recruitment toward underrepresented minorities who are committed to Boston Public Schools. The program does not focus on specific certification areas, but rather tries to recruit and prepare teachers who will remain in the Boston Public Schools. To this end, they provide an extensive internship in the schools and course work that is explicitly tied to Boston's "features of effective teaching." The Chicago Residency program, in contrast, is run by a not-for-profit organization, the Academy for Urban School Leadership, also in concert with the Chicago Public Schools and National-Louis University.[12] Like the Boston program, this program is specifically tailored to prepare teachers who will remain in Chicago Public Schools.

Other district-run programs, such as the Los Angeles Unified School District internship program and the New York City Teaching Fellows, lack the extended field experience provided in these residency models. While they are similar to the Boston residency program in the nature of their provider, our first dimension, they differ from the residency programs along our fourth dimension, the timing and focus of course-work and fieldwork preparation. While the Boston program targets diversity and retention, the California and New York programs tend to focus more on filling high-needs fields and difficult-to-staff schools with teachers who have strong academic backgrounds (dimensions 2 and 3).

New Jersey's alternative route provides an interesting example of a well-established program with a somewhat different profile.[13] One of the first early-entry routes, New Jersey's Provisional Teacher Program began in 1985 and is state-run (dimension 1), though it is a mixed model in that it utilizes IHEs for much of its course-work requirements for teachers once they begin teaching, and it also relies on districts for mentoring and evaluation. The New Jersey program initially recruited only individuals with bachelor's degrees outside of education and used interviews and test scores to demonstrate subject-matter knowledge as selection criteria (dimension 2). More recently it has also targeted candidates for vocational education who may not hold a bachelor's degree. The program aimed to fill vacancies in difficult-to-staff schools and fields including math, science, and special education (dimension 3). Similar to other early-entry routes, the timing of course work marks a substantial divergence from traditional programs, with teachers covering the vast majority of the course work after beginning teaching (dimension 4). The New Jersey program has distinguished itself not only because it was one of the first large alternative certification programs, but also because it provides a large number of teachers (approximately 40% of all new teachers in New Jersey). This program has successfully increased both the diversity and the average academic ability of New Jersey teachers, and its teachers have even higher retention rates than other teachers in the state. Statistics about their effectiveness at improving student test scores is not available.

As is clear from these examples, not only are there a variety of different programs, but the variation across dimensions provides different subgroups of programs within the broad umbrella of alternative certification. In conducting comparisons to determine relative effectiveness, it makes little sense to compare the broad categories of *alternative* and *traditional*. Instead, it makes more sense to compare programs that differ with respect to key dimensions. Therefore, we might compare programs with yearlong internships to those with minimal field experience; those that are district-run to those that are university-run; or those that target individuals with strong academic credentials to those that target individuals with ties to the community. It is through these types of comparisons that we are more likely to learn about the merits of different approaches and thus be able to improve the recruitment and preparation of teachers.

IMPLICATIONS FOR PRACTICE

As many of the chapters in this volume suggest, it is high time to move away from the argument over which pathway should predominate in the preparation of teachers. Rather, we should learn from the successes and challenges of the diversity of programs currently available and from additional experimentation in our efforts to improve teaching, particularly in the urban settings where alternative certification programs often take root.

Alternative routes took off, in part, because colleges and universities were relatively unresponsive to the needs of districts, particularly their difficulties in staffing certain subject areas and schools serving high-needs students. The proliferation of alternative certification programs in response to district needs demonstrates the important link between teacher recruitment and preparation, on one hand, and the job market for teachers on the other. It is an obvious link but one that traditional university-based teacher-preparation programs appear to have lost sight of. Part of the appeal of district-based programs is that they are often designed to fulfill local workforce needs. The importance of the link to the districts doesn't stop, however, with filling vacancies. A closer connection between those that prepare teachers and those that hire them allows teacher candidates to learn about curriculum and instructional practices they are likely to see in the classroom, helping to prepare them for particular school contexts and curricula.

District-run programs are more practical in large urban areas that require large-enough numbers of teachers on an annual basis; these kinds of labor markets enable the economies of scale necessary for a district to run a preparation program efficiently. However, the link between providers and employers can be accomplished in multiple ways. Collaborations among districts, as well as collaborations between districts or charter-management organizations and other institutions—whether they be universities or private organizations—can still provide a channel through which preparation programs can learn about districts' needs and contexts and then develop or adjust their program accordingly to address those needs.

This important role for districts does not necessarily mean the end to university-based teacher-preparation programs. In fact, a large number of alternative-route programs, including Teach For America, the New Jersey Provisional Teacher Program, and the New York City Teaching Fellows, rely heavily on universities to provide course work, supervision, and other services for teacher candidates. It would take huge capacity building for these alternative routes to be self-sufficient; as the relevant expertise may be available locally, it may make more sense to develop partnerships that bridge different realms of expertise. However, for universities to continue to be viable partners in this work, they will need to learn to be more adaptive to local needs. In addition, programs of all stripes need to make better use of data to improve the preparation of teachers. The long-term sustainability of these programs is likely to be secure only to the extent to which these programs make use of current knowledge of practices that are most effective in preparing and supporting new teachers, so that they engage in continuous improvement of their programs, building on the best features and eliminating those that are ineffective.

Research on multiple pathways also suggests that although there is a great diversity in the timing of course work taken by teachers prepared through different routes, there is relatively little variation in the content of course work across programs, especially programs in the same state that are governed by the same certification requirements. The lack of variation makes it difficult to research the impact of particular courses on teachers' practice or student achievement, and, in the long run, will make it harder to learn how to improve preparation.

We also learn from the existing research that one size is unlikely to fit all, either in fashion or teacher preparation. Just as responsiveness to local districts is important, so, too, is responsiveness to the pool of potential teachers that the program is drawing on. Programs that are responsive to the particular characteristics and backgrounds of different populations of prospective teachers and the differing contexts in which they might work are likely to be more effective and efficient in providing high-quality teachers to schools. Paraprofessionals entering certification programs, for example, may be very familiar with local schools but may need extended opportunities to think about content and how to teach it. In contrast, programs that recruit nationally, such as Teach For America or Teaching Fellows, might need to make a concerted effort to educate their participants about local schools. Similarly, programs that provide only minimal preservice preparation might need to refocus their efforts on what matters most for novice teachers; providing the same program, in the same order, to those who have several years before they take over as teacher of record, as well as those who will assume full responsibility for a classroom after just six weeks of summer school, ignores the differing needs of these groups. Similarly, teachers that have minimal opportunities to assume responsibilities for teaching during preservice preparation may need intensive coaching and support during the first months of full-time teaching. Tailoring programs to specific contexts and to the characteristics of participants will ensure stronger preparation for all.

Finally, the existence of alternative routes has shown that we can recruit a talented pool of individuals interested in teaching. Programs such as Teach For America and The New Teacher Project have done a fabulous job of making undergraduates aware of teaching. By increasing the pool of people who apply to such programs, they are able to be much more selective, along multiple dimensions, including content knowledge, leadership, persistence, and a range of other characteristics. Unlike university providers of teacher education, who may wait for students to find them, these programs aggressively recruit—on college campuses, on New York subways, in national magazines. In addition, by reducing the preservice course-work requirements—often simply moving those requirements into the first years of teaching—these programs have also made it possible for teachers to enter classrooms quickly. This combination of recruitment and reduction of entry costs has provided these programs with a fundamentally different pool of teachers. The ability to recruit a broader pool of applicants into the classroom, however, is of benefit only to the extent that it improves the opportunities and outcomes of students. Future research will need to continue to explore the best combination of recruitment strategies, selection criteria, preservice preparation, and ongoing support that will produce the most effective teachers.

DIRECTIONS FOR FUTURE RESEARCH

Need for Greater Experimentation

As we and others have noted, many alternative-route programs are hardly distinguishable from more-traditional programs, in terms of the substance of preparation.[14] Candidates enrolled in many alternative-route programs take very similar courses to those taken by candidates enrolled in traditional, university-based programs. What differs is the timing of when they are likely to encounter these courses. In part, this reflects the existence of state and national standards that regulate the content of professional preparation programs. However, the standards do not generally dictate how such content should be taught or the sequencing of content. While it might make sense for students in more-traditional programs to consider the aims and purposes of education in a democratic society at the beginning of their yearlong (or multiyear) programs, it seems to make much less sense to frontload this material in a six-week summer experience, knowing that candidates will take over classrooms in September. Similarly, given the importance of learning to manage classrooms so that teaching and learning are possible, programs with abbreviated field experience might need to spend even more time on this aspect of teaching during preservice preparation, and also, to design mentoring programs to help novices develop effective routines and interactions with students in the very first weeks of school. Intensive support early on might prevent problems from occurring later.

In surveying the landscape of teacher education in New York City, we were struck equally by the proliferation of programs and the lack of true variation in content that characterized these programs. We argued:

> Finally . . . the field [of teacher education] may need to develop greater incentives for experimentation. As organizational theory

suggests, while institutions must balance experimentation with conservation to flourish, many of the existing incentives favor the more conservative course (March, 1991). This may be particularly true in the highly regulated context of teacher education. The current press to evaluate teacher education programs through their impact on graduates' impact on student learning, however, may represent one opportunity to link experimentation with accountability through the design of more imaginative programs that are carefully studied in terms of impact. Programs might be freed from state regulations, much as charter schools are, to develop experimental models that systematically vary features of preparation and study the results. For example, teacher educators might create some dramatically different versions of the preservice summer component of early-entry routes with regard to the design of both field experiences and course work and then follow teachers across the first few years of teaching. Similarly, teacher educators might develop innovative college-recommending programs as part of a design experiment, in which variations in format are carefully planned and then studied systematically over several years. Such design experiments could make use of the proliferation of programs that already exists to learn more about how best to prepare teachers for particular contexts, students, or subject areas.

There are many dimensions of teacher education along which to experiment. Many of the current alternative certification programs provide significant variations in recruitment and selection; future research might extend this area. For example, what are the personality traits, experiences, and skills that are associated with more-effective teaching, particularly in the early years? How can we better identify prospective teachers who bring some of these traits into the classroom?

We might also design experiments around curricular and instructional approaches in preservice preparation. While there are very few studies that provide evidence of the link between features of teacher preparation and student outcomes, one recent paper finds that opportunities to practice the tasks of teaching during preservice course work—such as assessing and reviewing students' work or teaching a guided reading lesson—is associated with greater value-added to student test performance.[15] Using the summer institutes provided by many alternative-route programs, researchers could experiment with approaches to preparation that are closely linked to practice. A number of researchers in teacher education are beginning to experiment with the use of approximations of practice in university course work, including simulations and rehearsals of practice in which potential teachers respond to well-structured scenarios and learn ways of enacting instructional routines, or of responding to common situations and common difficulties.[16] Experimentation in this area linked with systematic collection of student outcome data could help to improve preparation in the future.

Respecting the Local Nature of Teacher Education

The chapters in this book also suggest a different way of exploring teacher education, looking not at individual programs nor at national samples, but rather at the range of programs that serve a common school district or labor market. Studies are currently investigating teacher education across entire states (c.f. Ohio's Teacher Quality Partnership, and studies of teacher education in Florida and Louisiana), as well as for particular districts (c.f. the Teacher Pathway Project in New York City). Such approaches allow researchers to describe more clearly the pool of potential teachers, the range of routes into teaching from which they have to choose, and how these factors interact. By looking at a single state, the researchers can better understand the policies and the political environment. Such approaches also respect the local nature of teacher education. What is true of New York, a highly regulated context for teacher education, is not necessarily true of Florida, where less regulation exists. This local perspective is critical in understanding both the constraints and possibilities facing teacher educators and school districts that seek to prepare and hire the next generation of teachers.

Future research will be more useful for improving teacher education—and teaching, more generally—if it continues to move away from merely looking at variation across pathways, and instead, looks for the individual features of those programs that have an impact on results. These important features—including high-quality supervision of student teaching, course work tied to the practice of teaching, and selection of applicants with given propensities or skills—can cut across pathways and programs, improving outcomes for both teachers and students. By understanding and incorporating these features, we will accelerate the improvement of all routes into teaching.

Conducting such research will require careful specification of features of preparation and support. We are just beginning the process of delineating and defining the dimensions of teacher preparation so that we can carefully compare across programs. For example, investigating the effects of mentoring requires specifying in greater detail those aspects of mentoring that might matter for teachers and differ across programs; these features may include the qualifications of mentors, the substantive focus of mentoring interactions, the resources (such as time) available for mentoring, and so forth. Each dimension of the different pathways to teaching has this same variability, whether it be the possible dimensions along which programs can target their recruitment and selection or the scope of content and pedagogy covered in course work for teachers of elementary mathematics.

We also need more research that looks at the interactions among person, program, and context, as suggested by chapters 3 and 4 in this volume. Research that explores the differential kinds of support and experiences required to help teachers with diverse profiles succeed in their first year of teaching could help providers tailor their programs to the specific needs of different pools of teachers. For example, how should the preservice summer experience for prospective teachers who bring strong subject-matter backgrounds but little teaching experience differ from the preparation of those who bring extensive experiences with youth but lack strong preparation in content? How should the course work for those who begin teaching after a short summer program differ from that offered to candidates who take a year of course work before teaching? How should the preparation for those who will teach in schools with a substantial proportion of students who are English-language learners differ from those who will teach in more English-dominant schools? The answers to such questions might lead to more variation in the course work provided to new entrants to teaching, not just the current variation in the timing of that course work. This variation across programs could, in turn, improve the preparation of teachers for the wide variety of teaching jobs in our diverse communities and schools.

Finally, as many have noted, teacher education cannot stop when a teacher first enters the classroom. It may, in fact, be difficult to accurately predict a teacher's strengths and weaknesses until he or she is faced with the actual task of teaching. This difficulty of predicting teachers' needs is likely to be even greater for teachers who enter the classroom with less extensive classroom experiences, or for those whose experiences in classrooms during their preparation were in teaching contexts quite different from the ones they face as full-time classroom teachers. Regardless of their pathway into teaching, teachers and their students can benefit from ongoing instructional support, especially in the first years of teaching. A critical area for both researchers and practitioners is how to structure those supports to best respond to what may be quite different needs of teachers across classrooms and schools.

Teaching is a complex task, drawing on many skills and requiring a range of knowledge about content, about students, and about how to communicate complex subject matter and motivate learning. Today's teachers enter the classroom through a diverse array of pathways, some with more focus on recruitment and selection and others with a greater emphasis on course work or structured experiences in schools prior to teaching. Such diversity in entry routes may be a good thing for schools and students; different routes may draw on a variety of sources for the skills needed in schools and allow for different preparation experiences for teachers with varying strengths. Yet, we are not learning as much from the proliferation of possible routes into teaching as we could. By carefully specifying the dimensions of teacher recruitment, selection, and preparation, and by collecting and analyzing information on the teaching practices and student outcomes of teachers from different pathways, we can learn much more than we know now about how to staff our classrooms most effectively. Experimentation and learning from our experiences, and the experiences across the country, may well be the key to better teaching and greater learning in the future.

Notes

INTRODUCTION
Pam Grossman and Susanna Loeb

1. See Emily Feistritzer, *Alternative Teacher Certification: A State by State Analysis 2007* (Washington, DC: National Center for Educational Information, 2008).
2. See Feistritzer, *Alternative Teacher Certification.*
3. See, for example, Linda Darling-Hammond, "The case for university-based teacher education" in Richard Roth (Ed.), *The Role of the University in the Preparation of Teachers* (London: Falmer Press, 1999) and Emily Feistritzer and Charlene K. Haar, *Alternate Routes to Teaching* (Upper Saddle River, NJ: Pearson Education, 2008) for differing sides of this argument.
4. See Hamilton Lankford, Susanna Loeb, and James Wyckoff, "Teacher Sorting and the Plight of Urban Schools: A Descriptive Analysis," *Educational Evaluation and Policy Analysis, 24*, No. 1 (2002): 37–62; Heather Peske and Kati Haycock, *Teaching Inequality: How Poor and Minority Students are Shortchanged on Teacher Quality* (Washington, DC: The Education Trust, 2006).
5. See, for example, Donald Boyd, Hamilton Lankford, Susanna Loeb, Jonah Rockoff, and James Wyckoff, "The Narrowing Gap in New York City Teacher Qualifications and its Implications for Student Achievement in High Poverty Schools," Teacher Policy Research Working Paper (Albany, NY: Teacher Policy Research, 2007), available online at http://www.teacherpolicyresearch.org/ResearchPapers/tabid/103/Default.aspx.
6. See Kenneth Zeichner and Elizabeth A. Hutchinson's chapter in this volume for a brief overview of this history. For a more extended history of this phenomena, see J. W. Fraser, *Preparing America's Teachers: A History* (New York: Teachers College Press, 2007).
7. See Feistritzer, *Alternative Teacher Certification*; Kenneth Zeichner and Hilary G. Conklin, "Teacher Education Programs," in Marilyn Cochran-Smith and Kenneth Zeichner (Eds.), *Studying Teacher Education* (Mahwah, NJ: Lawrence Erlbaum, 2005); Daniel C. Humphrey and Marjorie E. Wechsler, "Insights into Alternative Certification: Initial Findings from a National Study," *Teachers College Record, 109*, No. 3 (2007): 483–530.
8. See Gary Natriello and Karen Zumwalt, "New Teachers for Urban Schools? The Contribution of the Provisional Teacher Program in New Jersey," *Education and Urban*

Society, 26, No. 1 (1993): 49–62; Trish Stoddard and Robert Floden, "Traditional and Alternative Routes to Teacher Certification: Issues, Assumptions, and Misconceptions," in Kenneth Zeichner, Susan Melnick, and Mary-Louise Gomez (Eds.), *Currents of Reform in Pre-Service Teacher Education* (New York: Teachers College Press, 1996).

9. National Center for Alternative Certification, "Alternative Teacher Certification: A State by State Analysis," available online at http://www.teach-now.org/overview.cfm.

10. Feistritzer, *Alternative Teacher Certification.*

11. Feistritzer and Harr, *Alternate Routes to Teaching*; Zeichner and Conklin, "Teacher Education Programs."

12. See Zeichner and Conklin, "Teacher Education Programs," for a discussion of the different ways in which alternative certification has been defined. See also Willis D. Hawley, "The Theory and Practice of Alternative Certification: Implications for the Improvement of Teaching," *Peabody Journal of Education, 67*, No. 3 (1990): 3–34.

13. See Kate Walsh and Sandi Jacobs, "Alternative Certification Isn't Alternative" (Washington, DC: Thomas B. Fordham Institute and National Council on Teacher Quality, 2007) for a discussion of this point.

14. See Donald Boyd, Pam Grossman, Hamilton Lankford, Susanna Loeb, and James Wyckoff, "Complex by Design: Investigating Pathways into Teaching in New York City Schools," *Journal of Teacher Education, 57*, No. 2 (2006): 155–166.

15. See Jason A. Grissom's chapter in this volume for a discussion of this issue. See also Susanna Loeb, Linda Darling-Hammond, and John Luczak, "How Teaching Conditions Predict Teacher Turnover in California Schools," *Peabody Journal of Education, 80*, No. 3 (2005): 44–70; Katherine O. Strunk and Joseph P. Robinson, "Oh, Won't You Stay: A Multilevel Analysis of the Difficulties in Retaining Qualified Teachers," *Peabody Journal of Education, 81*, No. 4 (2006): 65–94.

16. See Donald Boyd, Pam Grossman, Hamilton Lankford, Susanna Loeb, and James Wyckoff, "How Changes in Entry Requirements Alter the Teacher Workforce and Affect Student Achievement," *Education Finance and Policy, 1*, No. 2 (2006): 176–216; Thomas J. Kane, Jonah E. Rockoff, and Douglas O. Staiger, *What Does Certification Tell Us About Teacher Effectiveness? Evidence from New York City*, NBER Working Paper 12155 (Cambridge, MA: National Bureau of Economic Research, 2006); Humphrey and Wechsler, *Insights in Alternative Certification*; Walsh and Jacobs, *Alternative Certification Isn't Alternative*; Zeichner and Conklin, "Teacher Education Programs."

17. See Linda Darling-Hammond and Barnett Berry, "Recruiting Teachers for the 21st Century: The Foundation for Educational Equity," *Journal of Negro Education, 68*, No. 3 (1999): 254–279.

18. See Paul Decker, Daniel P. Mayer, and Steven Glazerman, *The Effects of Teach For America on Students: Findings from a National Evaluation* (Princeton, NJ: Mathematica Policy Research, Inc., 2004); Linda Darling-Hammond, Deborah J. Holtzman, Su Jin Gatlin, and Julian Vasquez Heilig, "Does Teacher Preparation Matter?

Evidence about Teacher Certification, Teach For America, and Teacher Effectiveness," *Education Policy Analysis Archives, 13,* No. 42 (2005), available online at http://epaa.asu.edu/epaa/v13n42/.

CHAPTER 1
THE DEVELOPMENT OF ALTERNATIVE CERTIFICATION POLICIES
AND PROGRAMS IN THE UNITED STATES
Kenneth Zeichner and Elizabeth A. Hutchinson

1. David L. Angus and Jeffrey Mirel, *Professionalism and the Public Good: A Brief History of Teacher Certification* (Washington, DC: Thomas Fordham Foundation, 2001), available online at http://www.edexcellence.net/doc/angus.pdf; James W. Fraser, *Preparing America's Teachers: A History* (New York: Teachers College Press, 2007); and Christopher J. Lucas, *Teacher Education in America* (New York: St. Martins, 1999).
2. Fraser, *Preparing America's Teachers,* p. 216.
3. Fraser, *Preparing America's Teachers,* p. 92.
4. Lawrence A. Baines, "Deconstructing Teacher Certification," *Phi Delta Kappan, 88,* No. 4 (2006): 326–329; Lawrence A. Baines, "The Transmogrification of Teacher Education," *The Teacher Educator, 42,* No. 2 (2006): 140–156.
5. A survey of 2007 graduates of California teacher-education programs conducted in May and June 2007 indicated that about 27 percent of the 2,585 respondents completed their student teaching or internship experiences as teachers of record in California classrooms (personal communication with David Wright, California State University Chancellor's Office, October 2007).
6. For the first point, see Margaret Spellings, *The Secretary's Fifth Annual Report on Teacher Quality* (Washington, DC: U.S. Department of Education), available online at www.title2.org. For figures on numbers of teachers prepared through alternative routes, see Emily Feistritzer and Charlene K. Haar, *Alternate Routes to Teaching* (Upper Saddle River, NJ: Pearson Education, 2008)
7. Michael Sedlak, "Competing Visions of Purpose, Practice, and Policy" in Marilyn Cochran-Smith, Sharon Feiman-Nemser, and John McIntyre (Eds.), *Handbook of Research on Teacher Education,* 3rd ed. (Mahwah, NJ: Lawrence Erlbaum, 2008), 863.
8. David Imig and Scott Imig, "From Traditional Certification to Competitive Certification," in Marilyn Cochran-Smith, Sharon Feiman-Nemser, and John McIntyre (Eds.), *Handbook of Research on Teacher Education,* 3rd ed. (Mahwah, NJ: Lawrence Erlbaum, 2008), 886–907.
9. For a discussion of client-centered certification, see Kate Walsh, "A Candidate-Centered Model for Teacher Preparation and Licensure," in Frederick Hess, Andrew Rotherham, and Kate Walsh (Eds.), *A Qualified Teacher in Every Classroom?* (Cambridge, MA: Harvard Education Press, 2004), 223–254. See Sedlak, "Competing Visions of Purpose, Practice, and Policy."

10. Gary Fenstermacher, "The Place of Alternative Certification in the Education of Teachers" in *Peabody Journal of Education, 67*, No. 3 (1990): 155.

11. Nancy E. Adelman, *An Exploratory Study of Teacher Alternative Certification and Retraining Programs* (Washington, DC: U.S. Department of Education, 1986); Barnett Berry, "Quality Alternatives in Teacher Education: Dodging the Silver Bullet and Doing What's Right for Students," *The State Education Standard, 1*, No. 2 (2000): 21–25; Kenneth Zeichner and Hilary Conklin, "Research on Teacher Education Programs" in Marilyn Cochran-Smith and Kenneth Zeichner (Eds.), *Studying Teacher Education* (Mahwah, NJ: Lawrence Erlbaum, 2005), 645–736.

12. Emily Feistritzer, *Preparing Teachers for the Classroom: The Role of the Higher Education Act and No Child Left Behind* (testimony presented to the Subcommittee on Higher Education, Lifelong Learning and Competitiveness, Committee on Education and Labor, U.S. House of Representatives, May 17, 2007); Kate Walsh and Sandi Jacobs, *Alternative Certification Isn't Alternative* (Washington, DC: Thomas B. Fordham Institute and National Council on Teacher Quality, 2007); Kenneth Zeichner and Ann K. Schulte, "What We Know and Don't Know from Peer Reviewed Research about Alternative Teacher Certification," *Journal of Teacher Education, 52*, No. 4 (2001): 266–282.

13. Several categories in Feistritzer's classification system refer to alternative routes based primarily in institutions of higher education. This database, which is guided by how the individual states define alternative routes, is widely considered to be the most thorough and accurate tabulation of state policies with regard to alternative routes to teaching.

14. Richard J. Coley and Margaret E. Thorpe, *A Look at the MAT Model of Teacher Education and its Graduates: Lessons for Today* (Princeton, NJ: Educational Testing Service, 1986).

15. Harold Benjamin, "The 5-Year Curriculum for Prospective Teachers," *Educational Administration and Supervision, 19*, No. 1 (1933): 1–6.

16. Irving G. Hendrick, "Academic Revolution in California," *Southern California Quarterly 49*, Nos. 2, 3, 4 (1967): 127–166, 253–295, 359–406.

17. Robert B. Howsam, Dean C. Corrigan, George W. Denemark, and Robert J. Nash, *Educating a Profession* (New York: John Wiley, 1976); Holmes Group, *Tomorrow's Teachers* (East Lansing: Michigan State University College of Education, 1986); Carnegie Forum on Education and the Economy, *A Nation Prepared: Teachers for the 21st Century* (New York: Carnegie Corporation, 1986).

18. Emily Feistritzer, *The Making of a Teacher: A Report on Teacher Preparation in the U.S.* (Washington, DC: National Center for Education Information, 1999).

19. Baines, "Deconstructing Teacher Certification"(a); "The Transmogrification of Teacher Education" (b); Robert G. Holland, *To Build a Better Teacher: The Emergence of a Competitive Education Industry* (Westport, CT: Praeger, 2004).

20. Donald Boyd, Pam Grossman, Karen Hammerness, Hamilton Lankford, Susanna Loeb, et al., *Surveying the Landscape of Teacher Education in New York City: Con-*

strained Variation and the Challenge of Motivation (2007, August), retrieved from www.teacherpolicyresearch.org on October 31, 2007.

21. Zeichner and Conklin, "Research on Teacher Education Programs."

22. Trish Stoddart and Robert E. Floden, "Traditional and Alternative Routes to Teacher Certification: Issues, Assumptions, and Misconceptions," in Kenneth Zeichner, Susan Melnick, and Mary-Louise Gomez (Eds.), *Currents of Reform in Pre-Service Teacher Education* (New York: Teachers College Press, 1996); Willis D. Hawley, "The Theory and Practice of Alternative Certification: Implications for the Improvement of Teaching," *Peabody Journal of Education, 67,* No. 3 (1990); Linda Darling-Hammond and John Bransford (Eds.), *Preparing Teachers for a Changing World* (San Francisco: Jossey-Bass, 2005).

23. The empirical evidence related to these various assumptions will be addressed in the other chapters of this book.

24. Linda Darling-Hammond, "Teaching and Knowledge: Policy Issues Posed by Alternative Certification for Teachers," *Peabody Journal of Education, 67,* No. 3 (1992): 123–154; Vicky S. Dill, "Alternative Teacher Certification," in John Sikula (Ed.), *Handbook of Research on Teacher Education,* 2nd ed. (New York: Macmillan, 1996), 932–960; Stoddart and Floden, "Traditional and Alternative Routes to Teacher Certification: Issues, Assumptions, and Misconceptions."

25. Willis D. Hawley, "The Theory and Practice of Alternative Certification: Implications for the Improvement of Teaching," *Peabody Journal of Education, 67,* No. 3 (1990): 4.

26. Feistritzer and Haar, *Alternate Routes to Teaching,* p. 11. Using NCES data, the authors assert that of the individuals who received bachelor's degrees in 1999–2000 and who were certified to teach, 23 percent were not teaching within a year of graduating.

27. Ana M. Villegas and Tamara F. Lucas, "Diversifying the Teacher Workforce: A Retrospective and Prospective Analysis," in Mark A. Smylie and Debra Miretzky (Eds.), *Developing the Teacher Workforce* (Chicago: University of Chicago Press, 2004), 70–114.

28. Martin Haberman and Linda Post, "Teachers for Multicultural Schools: The Power of Selection," *Theory into Practice, 37,* No. 2 (1998): 97–104.

29. Feistritzer and Haar, *Alternate Routes to Teaching.*

30. Martin Haberman, "Alternative Teacher Certification," *Action in Teacher Education, 8,* No. 2 (1986): 13–18.

31. J. Bliss, "Alternative Teacher Certification in Connecticut: Reshaping the Profession," *Peabody Journal of Education, 67,* No. 3 (1990): 35–54; R. Wisniewski, "Alternative Programs and the Reform of Teacher Education," *Action in Teacher Education, 8,* No. 2 (1986): 37–44.

32. E. Eubanks and R. Parish, "Why Does the Status Quo Persist?" *Phi Delta Kappan, 72,* No. 3 (1990): 196–197; National Center for Education Statistics, *The Condition of Education* (Washington, DC: U.S. Department of Education, 2004); Heather G. Peske and Kati Haycock, *Teaching Inequality: How Poor and Minority*

Children Are Shortchanges on Teacher Quality (Washington, DC: Education Trust, June 2006).

33. Frederick M. Hess, *Tear Down the Wall: The Case for a Radical Overhaul of Teacher Certification* (Washington, DC: Progressive Policy Institute, 2001); Walsh, "A Candidate-Centered Model for Teacher Preparation and Licensure."

34. Naomi Schaefer, "Traditional and Alternative Certification: A View from the Trenches," in Marci Kanstoroom and Chester Finn (Eds.), *Better Teachers, Better Schools* (Washington, DC: Thomas Fordham Foundation, 1999), 137–162.

35. Linda Darling-Hammond, "The Case for University-Based Teacher Education," in Robert A. Roth (Ed.), *The Role of the University in the Preparation of Teachers,* (London: Falmer Press, 1999), 8–24; Arthur E. Wise, "Choosing between Professionalism and Amateurism," *The Educational Forum, 58*, No. 2 (1994): 139–146.

36. Arthur E. Bestor, "On the Education and Certification of Teachers," *School and Society* 78 (1953): 81–87.

37. Bestor, "On the Education and Certification of Teachers," p. 87. These claims about the alleged low academic quality of professional education courses have existed for a long time, but are based on little or no direct study of teacher-education programs. Kenneth M. Zeichner, *Understanding the Character and Quality of the Academic and Professional Components of Teacher Education,* Issue paper #88-1 (East Lansing, MI: National Center for Research on Teacher Learning, College of Education, Michigan State University, 1988); Zeichner and Conklin, "Research on Teacher Education Programs," p. 87.

38. Baines, "Deconstructing Teacher Certification; The Transmogrification of Teacher Education."

39. Robert Kuttner, *Everything for Sale: The Virtues and Limits of Markets* (Chicago: University of Chicago Press, 1999).

40. Patricia H. Hinchey and Karen Cadiero-Kaplan, "The Future of Teacher Education and Teaching: Another Piece of the Privatization Puzzle," *Journal for Critical Educational Policy Studies, 3*, No. 2 (2005), available online at www.jceps.com; Jacqueline Raphael and Sheila Tobias, "Profit-Making or Profiteering? Proprietaries Target Teacher Education," *Change, 29*, No. 6 (1997): 44–49.

41. Katharine C. Lyall and Kathleen R. Sell, *The True Genius of America at Risk: Are We Losing Our Public Universities to De Facto Privatization?* (Westport, CT: Praeger, 2006).

42. Frederick M. Hess, "Break the Link," *Education Next, 2*, No. 1 (2002): 22–28, available online at http://www.hoover.org/publications/ednext; Imig and Imig, "From Traditional Certification to Competitive Certification."

43. Hess, "Break the Link," p. 980.

44. See http://www.teach-now.org.

45. Rod Paige, *Meeting the Highly Qualified Teachers Challenge: The Secretary's Annual Report on Teacher Quality* (Washington, DC: U.S. Department of Education, 2002), 40.

46. Emily Feistritzer and Charlene K. Haar, *Alternate Routes to Teaching* (Upper Saddle River, NJ: Pearson Education, 2008), 109.

47. Emily Feistritzer, *Alternative Teacher Certification: A State by State Analysis 2007* (Washington, DC: National Center for Education Information, 2008).
48. Feistritzer and Haar, *Alternate Routes to Teaching*.
49. Willis D. Hawley and Andrew Wayne, in press. All of the states that have approved ABCTE require mentoring during the early years of teaching, but only one, Mississippi, requires the completion of any training or course work (http://www. abcte.org).
50. Adelman, *An Exploratory Study of Teacher Alternative Certification and Retraining Programs*; Sheila Nataraj Kirby, Linda Darling-Hammond, and Lisa Hudson, "Nontraditional Recruits to Mathematics and Science Teaching," *Educational Evaluation and Policy Analysis, 11*, No. 3 (1989): 301–323; Daniel C. Humphrey and Marjorie E. Wechsler, "Insights into Alternative Certification: Initial Findings from a National Study, *Teachers College Record, 109*, No. 3 (2007): 483–530; Daniel C. Humphrey, Marjorie E. Wechsler, and Heather J. Hough, "Characteristics of effective alternative teacher certification programs," *Teachers College Record, 110*, No. 4 (2008): 1–63; Feistritzer and Haar, *Alternate Routes to Teaching*.
51. Feistritzer and Haar, *Alternate Routes to Teaching*.
52. Zeichner and Conklin, "Research on Teacher Education Programs."
53. S. Wilson and E. Tamir, "The Evolving Field of Teacher Education, in M. Cochran-Smith, S. Nemser, and D. J. McIntyre (Eds.), *Handbook of Research on Teacher Education, 2nd ed.* (Mahwah, NJ: Erlbaum, 2008), pp. 908–935.
54. For example, Linda Darling-Hammond, one of the most prominent advocates for college- and university-based teacher preparation has called for the creation of new alternative routes to attract mid-career individuals and others who want to enter teaching (Education Commission of the States, 2000). The kinds of alternative routes that she and advocates for the deregulation of teacher education would accept are different, but the support for multiple pathways cuts across the political spectrum. Education Commission for the States, *Two Paths to Quality Teachers* (Denver: Author, June 2000).
55. There is also a belief by some that the continued existence of both early-entry and college-recommending pathways into teaching will lead to an effect on college and university programs of including more school-based experiences and an effect on early-entry experiences of including more professional education knowledge in their curricula. Fenstermacher, "The Place of Alternative Certification."
56. Marilyn Cochran-Smith and Kenneth Zeichner (Eds.), *Studying Teacher Education*, (Mahwah, NJ: Lawrence Erlbaum, 2005); Lyall and Sell, *The True Genius of America at Risk: Are We Losing Our Public Universities to De Facto Privatization?*; Kenneth Zeichner and Laura Paige, "The Current Status and Possible Future for 'Traditional' College and University-Based Teacher Education Programs in the U.S," in Thomas L. Good (Ed.), *21st Century Education: a Reference Handbook*, (Thousand Oaks, CA: Sage, in press).
57. See, for example, Linda Darling-Hammond, *Powerful Teacher Education* (San Francisco: Jossey-Bass, 2006).

58. Zeichner and Paige, "The Current Status and Possible Future for 'Traditional' College- and University-Based Teacher Education Programs in the U.S."
59. In 2007 the federal government underfunded "No Child Left Behind" by $15.8 billion and Title 1 by $12.2 billion (available online at http://www.nea.org).

CHAPTER 2
WHO GOES INTO EARLY-ENTRY PROGRAMS?
Karen Hammerness and Michelle Reininger

1. Marilyn Cochran-Smith and Mary Kim Fries, "Sticks, Stones, and Ideology: The Discourse of Reform in Teacher Education," *Educational Researcher, 30*, No. 8 (2001): 3–16; Kenneth M. Zeichner, "The Adequacies and Inadequacies of Three Current Strategies to Recruit, Prepare, and Retain the Best Teachers for All Students," *Teachers College Record, 105*, No. 3 (2003): 490–519.
2. Michael Kwiatkowski, "Debating Alternative Certification: A Trial by Achievement," in Marci Kanstoroom and Chester Finn Jr. (Eds.), *Better Teachers, Better Schools* (Washington, DC: Thomas B. Fordham Foundation, 1999): 215–238.
3. Early-entry pathways and programs designed to attract different populations of teachers have, in fact, been around for more than forty years. For instance, in the 1960s, an early-entry teacher-education program called the Teacher Corps was legislated with the intention of improving the education of "disadvantaged" students by recruiting bright, liberal arts graduates to teach in public schools serving poor and minority children. Bethany Rogers, "Broadening the Framework: Teaching as Activism in the National Teacher Corps" (paper presented at the annual meeting of the American Educational Research Association, San Diego, CA, April 12–16, 2004).
4. For description of the overall project, see Donald Boyd, Pam Grossman, Hamilton Lankford, Susanna Loeb, and James Wyckoff, "Complex by Design: Investigating Pathways into Teaching in New York City Schools," *Journal of Teacher Education, 57*, No. 2 (2006): 155–166.
5. Gregory A. Strizek, Jayme L. Pittsonberger, Kate E. Riordan, Deanna M. Lyter, and Greg F. Orlofsky, *Characteristics of Schools, Districts, Teachers, Principals, and School Libraries in the United States: 2003–04 Schools and Staffing Survey*, NCES 2006-313 Revised (U.S. Department of Education, National Center for Education Statistics. Washington, DC: U.S. Government Printing Office, 2006).
6. Thomas S. Dee, "Teachers and the Gender Gaps in Student Achievement," *The Journal of Human Resources, 42*, No. 3 (2007): 528–554.
7. Altogether across all populations, the survey of 2,647 teachers had a response rate of 35 percent. Emily Feistritzer, *Profile of Alternate Route Teachers* (Washington, DC: National Center for Education Information, 2005).
8. Feistritzer, *Profile of Troops to Teachers*, focuses on data from the TTT cohort. She notes that 82 percent of the sample are male. The Troops to Teachers sample size was 1,434, with a response rate of 48.4 percent.

9. Boyd et al., "Complex by Design: Investigating Pathways into Teaching in New York City Schools."

10. The programs included in their study were the following: the Teacher Education Institute in Elk Grove (CA) Unified School District, Milwaukee's Metropolitan Multicultural Teacher Education Program (MMTEP), North Carolina's NC TEACH, the New Jersey Provisional Teacher Program, the New York City Teaching Fellows Program, Teach For America, and the Texas Region XIII Education Service Center's Educator Certification Program. It is worth noting that one of the programs, MMTEP, is designed for paraprofessionals, which typically draws upon a different population than other early-entry programs. Daniel C. Humphrey and Marjorie E. Wechsler, "Insights into Alternative Certification: Initial Findings from a National Study," *Teachers College Record, 109*, No. 3 (2007): 483–530.

11. National Center for Education Statistics, *Digest of Education Statistics 2002* (Washington, DC: U.S. Department of Education, 2002), available online at http://nces.ed.gov/programs/digest/d02/tables/dt068.asp.

12. Jianping Shen, "Has the Alternative Certification Policy Materialized its Promise? A Comparison between Traditionally and Alternatively Certified Teachers in Public Schools," *Educational Evaluation and Policy Analysis, 19*, No. 3 (1997): 276–283.

13. Strizek et al., *Characteristics of Schools, Districts, Teachers, Principals, and School Libraries in the United States: 2003–04 Schools and Staffing Survey.*

14. Thomas S. Dee, "A Teacher Like Me: Does Race, Ethnicity, or Gender Matter?," *American Economic Association Papers and Proceedings, 95*, No. 2 (2005): 158–65.

15. "Other" category includes Native American or Alaskan Native, Asian, Native Hawaiian, or multiracial.

16. Feistritzer, *Profile of Alternate Route Teachers* (Washington, DC: National Center for Education Information, 2005); Feistritzer, *Profile of Troops to Teachers.*

17. Humphrey and Wechsler, "Insights into Alternative Certification: Initial Findings from a National Study."

18. Humphrey and Wechsler, "Insights into Alternative Certification: Initial Findings from a National Study," p. 496.

19. However, it is important to note that there is no evidence linking a teacher's age to effective teaching. Age is rather seen as providing insight into the career stage, amount of previous experience, and possible remaining years of employment in the workforce of an individual.

20. Stephen Provasnik and Scott Dorfman, *Mobility in the Teacher Workforce*, NCES 2005-114 (Washington, DC: U.S. Department of Education, National Center for Education Statistics. 2005), p. 3, available online at http://nces.ed.gov/pubsearch/pubsinfo.asp?pubid=2005114; Stephen Provasnik, personal communication to author, 2007.

21. One study estimated that by the age of thirty-two, the average American has worked for nine companies. Editors, "The Future of Work: Career Evolution," *The Economist* (2000, January 27).

22. Feistritzer, *Profile of Alternate Route Teachers.*

23. Feistritzer, *Profile of Alternate Route Teachers*, conducted an additional analysis of just the Troops to Teachers sample, and found that, in that sample, nine out of ten teachers were over forty years old. Since the TTT teachers made up 16 percent of her overall sample, they may have contributed to a higher overall average.

24. Humphrey and Wechsler, "Insights into Alternative Certification: Initial Findings from a National Study."

25. Humphrey and Wechsler, "Insights into Alternative Certification: Initial Findings from a National Study," p. 493.

26. Shen, "Has the Alternative Certification Policy Materialized its Promise? A Comparison between Traditionally and Alternatively Certified Teachers in Public Schools."

27. Elaine Chin and John Young, "A Person-Oriented Approach to Characterizing Beginning Teachers in Alternative Certification Programs." Educational Researcher, 36, No. 2 (2007): 74–83; Gary M. Crow, Linda Levine, and Nancy Nager, "No More Business as Usual: Career Changers Who Become Teachers," American Journal of Education, 98, No. 3 (1990): 197–223; Susan Moore Johnson, Finders and Keepers: Helping New Teachers Survive and Thrive in Our Schools (San Francisco: Jossey-Bass, 2004); Robert C. Serow and Krista D. Forrest, "Motives and Circumstances: Occupational-Change Experiences of Prospective Late-Entry Teachers," Teaching and Teacher Education, 10, No. 5 (1994): 555–563.

28. Crow, Levine, and Nager, "No More Business as Usual: Career Changers Who Become Teachers."

29. Chin and Young, "A Person-Oriented Approach to Characterizing Beginning Teachers in Alternative Certification Programs."

30. Johnson, *Finders and Keepers: Helping New Teachers Survive and Thrive in Our Schools*.

31. Chester Finn and Kathleen Madigan, "Removing the Barriers for Teacher Candidates," *Education Leadership, 58*, No. 8 (2001): 29–36.

32. Kwiatkowski, "Debating Alternative Certification: A Trial by Achievement."

33. Shen, "Has the Alternative Certification Policy Materialized its Promise? A Comparison between Traditionally and Alternatively Certified Teachers in Public Schools."

34. Elaine Chin, John Young, and Barry Floyd, "Placing Beginning Teachers in Hard-to-Staff Schools: Dilemmas Posed by Alternative Certification Programs" (paper presented at the annual meeting of the American Association of Colleges of Teacher Education, Chicago, IL, February 7–10, 2004); David Ruenzel, "Tortuous Routes" *Education Next, 2*, No. 1 (2002): 42–48, available online at http://media.hoover.org/documents/ednext20021_42.pdf.

35. Feistritzer, *Profile of Alternate Route Teachers*.

36. Johnson, *Finders and Keepers: Helping New Teachers Survive and Thrive in Our Schools*.

37. Johnson, *Finders and Keepers: Helping New Teachers Survive and Thrive in Our Schools*, notes that random sample surveys conducted in 2001–2002 by Project on the Next Generation of Teachers showed an "unexpectedly high proportion of

mid-career entrants to teaching: 47 percent in California, 46 percent in Massachusetts, 32 percent in Florida, and 28 percent in Michigan." However, she also notes that it is not clear whether these high proportions of mid-career entrants are the result of early-entry certification policies or not. On the other hand, the states with larger numbers of mid-career candidates also are states that have given considerable policy efforts to recruit mid-career candidates. Thus, programs especially designed to bring older entrants into teaching, such as the Massachusetts Initiative for New Teachers (MINT), the California Math and Science Teacher Initiative in California, and the Provisional Teacher Program in New Jersey, may have contributed at least in part to increases in older entrants in these states.

38. Karen Hammerness, "A First Look at Second Career Teachers" (Paper prepared for the Woodrow Wilson National Fellowship Foundation, 2007).

39. Humphrey and Wechsler, "Insights into Alternative Certification: Initial Findings from a National Study," p. 499.

40. Finn and Madigan, "Removing the Barriers for Teacher Candidates."

41. Susanna Loeb and Michelle Reininger, *Public Policy and Teacher Labor Markets: What We Know and Why it Matters* (East Lansing, MI: Michigan State University, Education Policy Center, 2004).

42. Daniel Goldhaber and Dominic Brewer, "Does Teacher Certification Matter? High School Teacher Certification Status and Student Achievement," *Education Evaluation and Policy Analysis, 22*, No. 2 (2000): 129–145.

43. Humphrey and Wechsler, "Insights into Alternative Certification: Initial Findings from a National Study."

44. Feistritzer, *Profile of Alternative Route Teachers.*

45. Feistritzer, *Profile of Troops to Teachers.*

46. Hammerness, "A First Look at Second Career Teachers."

47. Johnson, *Finders and Keepers: Helping New Teachers Survive and Thrive in Our Schools,* p. 15.

48. Feistritzer, *Profile of Alternate Route Teachers,* p. 15.

49. Humphrey and Wechsler, "Insights into Alternative Certification: Initial Findings from a National Study."

50. Humphrey and Wechsler, "Insights into Alternative Certification: Initial Findings from a National Study"; Johnson, *Finders and Keepers: Helping New Teachers Survive and Thrive in Our Schools.*

51. Robert C. Serow and Krista D. Forrest, "Motives and Circumstances: Occupational-Change Experiences of Prospective Late-Entry Teachers," Teaching and Teacher Education, 10, No. 5 (1994): 555–563.

52. Feistritzer, *Profile of Alternate Route Teachers.*

53. Johnson, *Finders and Keepers: Helping New Teachers Survive and Thrive in Our Schools.*

54. Humphrey and Wechsler, "Insights into Alternative Certification: Initial Findings from a National Study."

55. Humphrey and Wechsler, "Insights into Alternative Certification: Initial Findings from a National Study," p. 502.

56. Public Agenda, *Lessons Learned: New Teachers Talk About Their Jobs, Challenges and Long-Range Plans,* Issue No.2. "Working Without a Net: How New Teachers from Three Prominent Alternative Route Programs Describe Their First Year on the Job" (New York: Author, 2007), available online at www.publicagenda.org.

57. Gary Natriello and Karen Zumwalt, "Challenges to an Alternative Route for Teacher Education," in Ann Lieberman (Ed.), *The Changing Contexts of Teaching,* (Chicago: University of Chicago Press, 1992), 59–78.

58. Feistritzer, *Profile of Alternate Route Teachers*; Susan Moore Johnson, *Finders and Keepers: Helping New Teachers Survive and Thrive in Our Schools.*

59. Susan Moore Johnson, Sarah E. Birkeland, and Heather G. Peske, *A Difficult Balance: Incentives and Quality Control in Alternative Certification Programs* (Cambridge, MA: Project on the Next Generation of Teachers, 2005), available online at http://www.gse.harvard.edu/~ngt/Balance.pdf.

60. Feistritzer, *Profile of Alternate Route Teachers.*

61. Susan Moore Johnson and Edward Liu, "What Teaching Pays, What Teaching Costs" in *Finders and Keepers: Helping New Teachers Survive and Thrive in Our Schools,* ed. Susan Moore Johnson (San Francisco: Jossey-Bass, 2004); Clark R. Fowler, "The Massachusetts Signing Bonus Program for New Teachers: A Model for Teacher Preparation Worth Copying?," *Education Policy Analysis Archives, 11,* No. 13 (2003), available online at http://epaa.asu.edu/epaa/v11n13/.

62. Johnson and Liu, "What Teaching Pays, What Teaching Costs."

63. Johnson and Liu, "What Teaching Pays, What Teaching Costs," p. 225.

64. Edward Liu, Susan Moore Johnson, and Heather Peske, "New Teachers and the Massachusetts Signing Bonus: The Limits of Inducements," *Educational Evaluation and Policy Analysis, 26,* No. 3 (2004): 229.

65. Public Agenda, *Lessons Learned: New Teachers Talk About Their Jobs, Challenges and Long-Range Plans, Issue No. 2. Working Without a Net: How New Teachers from Three Prominent Alternative Route Programs Describe Their First Year on the Job* (New York: Author, 2007), available online at www.publicagenda.org.

66. Feistritzer, *Profile of Alternate Route Teachers.*

67. Feistritzer, *Profile of Alternate Route Teachers,* p. 20.

68. National Center for Education Statistics, *Digest of Education Statistics 2002* (Washington, DC: U.S. Department of Education, 2002), available online at http://nces.ed.gov/programs/digest/d02/tables/dt068.asp.

69. Feistritzer, *Profile of Alternate Route Teachers.*

70. Feistritzer, *Profile of Alternate Route Teachers,* p. 11.

71. Feistritzer, *Profile of Alternate Route Teachers,* p. 11.

72. Feistritzer, *Profile of Alternate Route Teachers,* p. 52.

73. Feistritzer, *Profile of Troops to Teachers.*

74. Clark R. Fowler, "The Massachusetts Signing Bonus Program for New Teachers: A Model for Teacher Preparation Worth Copying?"

75. Donald Boyd, Hamilton Lankford, Susanna Loeb, and James Wyckoff, "The Draw of Home: How Teachers' Preferences for Proximity Disadvantage Urban Schools,"

Journal of Policy Analysis and Management, 24, No. 1 (2005): 113–132; Johnson, *Finders and Keepers: Helping New Teachers Survive and Thrive in Our Schools*; Michelle Reininger, "Teachers' Location Preferences and the Implications for Schools with Different Student Populations" (paper presented at the Association for Public Policy Analysis and Management, Madison, WI, November 2006).

76. Boyd et al., "The Draw of Home: How Teachers Preferences for Proximity Disadvantage Urban Schools."
77. Reininger, "Teachers' Location Preferences and the Implications for Schools with Different Student Populations."
78. Johnson, *Finders and Keepers: Helping New Teachers Survive and Thrive in Our Schools.*
79. Feistritzer, *Profile of Alternate Route Teachers.*
80. Humphrey and Wechsler, "Insights into Alternative Certification: Initial Findings from a National Study."
81. Johnson, *Finders and Keepers: Helping New Teachers Survive and Thrive in Our Schools.*
82. "Teach For America Places Largest-Ever Corps, Expanding its Impact to 26 Regions Nationwide," accessed online at http://www.teachforamerica.org/newsroom/documents/081507_Largestcorps.htm.

CHAPTER 3
GETTING BEYOND THE LABEL: WHAT CHARACTERIZES ALTERNATIVE CERTIFICATION PROGRAMS?
Daniel C. Humphrey and Marjorie E. Wechsler

1. Emily Feistritzer, *Profile of Alternate Route Teachers* (Washington, DC: National Center for Education Information, 2005).
2. Daniel C. Humphrey and Marjorie E. Wechsler, "Insights into Alternative Certification: Initial Findings from a National Study, *Teachers College Record, 109,* No. 3 (2007):483–530.
3. Items measuring pedagogical content knowledge in reading/language arts and mathematics were drawn from a bank of items developed for the Study of Instructional Improvement being conducted by researchers at the University of Michigan (Deborah Ball, David Cohen, and Brian Rowan, principal investigators). See, for example: Heather C. Hill, Stephen G. Schilling, and Deborah L. Ball, "Developing Measures of Teachers' Mathematics Knowledge for Teaching," *Elementary School Journal, 105,* No. 1 (2004): 11–30; Geoffrey Phelps and Stephen G. Schilling, "Developing Measures of Content Knowledge for Teaching Reading," *Elementary School Journal, 105,* No. 1 (2004): 31–48.
4. Additional details on the programs and study methodology can be found in earlier publications available at http://policyweb.sri.com/cep/projects/display Project.jsp?Nick=altcert.

5. Willis D. Hawley, "The Theory and Practice of Alternative Certification: Implications for the Improvement of Teaching," in W. D. Hawley (Ed.), *The Alternative Certification of Teachers* (Teacher Education Monograph No. 14; Washington, DC: ERIC Clearinghouse on Teacher Education, 1992), pp. 3–34.

6. Suzanne M. Wilson, Robert E. Floden, and Joan Ferrini-Mundy, *Teacher Preparation Research: Current Knowledge, Gaps, and Recommendations* (Seattle, WA: University of Washington, Center for the Study of Teaching and Policy, 2001), available online at http://depts.washington.edu/ctpmail/PDFs/TeacherPrep-WFFM-02-2001.pdf; Kenneth M. Zeichner and Ann K. Schulte, "What We Know and Don't Know from Peer-Reviewed Research about Alternative Teacher Certification Programs," *Journal of Teacher Education, 52*, No. 4 (2001): 266–282.

7. Humphrey and Wechsler, "Insights into Alternative Certification: Initial Findings from a National Study."

8. Humphrey and Wechsler, "Insights into Alternative Certification: Initial Findings from a National Study."

9. Barron's Educational Services, Inc., *Profiles of American Colleges*, 25th ed. (Hauppauge, NY: Author, 2002).

10. Dale Ballou and Michael Podgursky, *Teacher Pay and Teacher Quality*. (Kalamazoo, MI: E. Upjohn Institute for Employment Research, 1997); Andrew J. Wayne and Peter Youngs, "Teacher Characteristics and Student Achievement Gains: A Review," *Review of Educational Research, 73*, No. 1 (2003): 89–122.

11. Humphrey and Wechsler, "Insights into Alternative Certification: Initial Findings From a National Study."

12. Some of the teaching experience reported by New Jersey teachers may have been caused by delays in their paperwork. The *Newark Star-Ledger* ("Teachers Held Up by State Logjam," October 5, 2004) reported more than 1,000 new teachers had experienced delays in receiving their teaching certificates. Presumably, some of these new teachers were in the alternative certification programs.

13. Humphrey and Wechsler, "Insights into Alternative Certification: Initial Findings From a National Study"; Susan Moore Johnson, Sarah E. Birkeland, and Heather G. Peske, *A Difficult Balance: Incentives and Quality Control in Alternative Certification Programs* (Cambridge, MA: The Project on the Next Generation of Teachers, 2005), available online at http://www.gse.harvard.edu/~ngt/balance.pdf.

14. Donald Boyd, Pam Grossman, Hamilton Lankford, and James Wyckoff, *How Changes in Entry Requirements Alter the Teacher Workforce and Affect Student Achievement* (Working Paper No. 11844; Washington, DC: National Bureau of Economic Research, 2005).

15. Thomas J. Kane, Jonah E. Rockoff, and Douglas O. Staiger, *What Does Certification Tell Us About Teacher Effectiveness? Evidence from New York City,* NBER Working Paper 12155 (Cambridge, MA: National Bureau of Economic Research, 2006).

16. Daniel C. Humphrey, Marjorie E. Wechsler, and Heather J. Hough, "Characteristics of Effective Alternative Teacher Certification Programs," *Teachers College Record, 110*, No. 4 (2008): 1–63.

CHAPTER 4
IS FAST-TRACK PREPARATION ENOUGH? IT DEPENDS
Susan Moore Johnson and Sarah E. Birkeland

1. Heather G. Peske conducted this research with us.
2. Daniel C. Humphrey, Marjorie E. Wechsler, Kristin Bosetti, Andrew Wayne, and Nancy Adelman, *Alternative Certification: Design for a National Study* (Menlo Park, CA, SRI International, 2002).
3. James Jelmberg, "College-Based Teacher Education versus State-Sponsored Alternative Programs," *Journal of Teacher Education, 47*, No. 1 (1996): 60–66; Martha N. Ovando and Mary B. Trube, "Capacity Building of Beginning Teachers from Alternative Certification Programs: Implications for Instructional Leadership," *Journal of School Leadership, 10*, No. 4 (2000): 346–366; Edith Guyton, M. C. Fox, and Kathleen A. Sisk, "Comparison of Teaching Attitudes, Teacher Efficacy, and Teacher Performance of First Year Teachers Prepared by Alternative and Traditional Teacher Education Programs," *Action in Teacher Education, 13*, No. 2 (1991): 1–9; John W. Miller, Michael C. McKenna, and Beverly A. McKenna, "A Comparison of Alternatively and Traditionally Prepared Teachers," *Journal of Teacher Education, 49*, No. 3 (1998): 165–176.
4. Daniel D. Goldhaber and Dominic J. Brewer, "Does Teacher Certification Matter? High School Teacher Certification Status and Student Achievement," *Educational Evaluation and Policy Analysis, 22*, No. 2 (2000): 129–145, 139.
5. Ildiko Laczko-Kerr and David Berliner, "The Effectiveness of Teach For America and Other Under-Certified Teachers on Student Academic Achievement: A Case of Harmful Public Policy," *Education Policy Analysis Archives, 10*, No. 37 (2002): 56.
6. Paul T. Decker, Daniel P. Mayer, and Steven Glazerman, *The Effects of Teach For America on Students: Findings from a National Evaluation* (Princeton, NJ: Mathematica Policy Research, Inc., 2004).
7. Linda Darling-Hammond, Deborah J. Holtzman, Su Jin Gatlin, and Julian V. Heilig, *Does Teacher Preparation Matter? Evidence about Teacher Certification, Teach For America, and Teacher Effectiveness* (Palo Alto: Stanford University, 2005).
8. G. Williamson McDiarmid and Suzanne M. Wilson, "An Exploration of the Subject Matter Knowledge of Alternate Route Teachers: Can We Assume They Know their Subject?," *Journal of Teacher Education, 42*, No. 2 (1991): 93–103.
9. Megan Tschannen-Moran, Anita Woolfolk Hoy, and Wayne K. Hoy, "Teacher Efficacy: Its Meaning and Measure," *Review of Educational Research, 68*, No. 2 (1998): 202–248; Frank W. Lutz, and Jerry B. Hutton, "Alternative Teacher Certification: Its Policy Implications for Classroom and Personnel Practice," *Educational Evaluation & Policy Analysis, 11*, No. 3 (1989): 237–254; Jelmberg, "College-Based Teacher Education versus State-Sponsored Alternative Programs"; Linda Darling-Hammond, Ruth Chung, and Frederick Frelow, "Variation in Teacher Preparation: How Well Do Different Pathways Prepare Teachers to Teach?," *Journal of Teacher Education, 53*, No. 4 (2002): 286–302; Edith Guyton, M. C. Fox, and Kathleen A. Sisk, "Comparison of Teaching Attitudes, Teacher Efficacy, and Teacher Per-

formance of First Year Teachers Prepared by Alternative and Traditional Teacher Education Programs"; John W. Miller, Michael C. Mckenna, and Beverly A. McKenna, "A Comparison of Alternatively and Traditionally Prepared Teachers."

10. Lora Cohen-Vogel and Thomas M. Smith, "Qualifications and Assignments of Alternatively Certified Teachers: Testing Core Assumptions," *American Educational Research Journal, 44*, No. 3 (2007): 732–753.

11. Daniel C. Humphrey and Marjorie E. Wechsler, "Insights into Alternative Certification: Initial Findings from a National Study," *Teachers College Record, 109*, No. 3 (2007): 483–530.

12. Suzanne M. Wilson, Robert E. Floden, and Joan Ferrini-Mundy, *Teacher Preparation Research: Current Knowledge, Gaps, and Recommendations* (Seattle, WA: University of Washington, Center for the Study of Teaching and Policy, 2001), available online at http://depts.washington.edu/ctpmail/PDFs/TeacherPrep-WFFM-02-2001.

13. Further information about the sample, methods, and findings of this study can be found in the full report, *A Difficult Balance: Incentives and Quality Control in Alternative Certification Programs*, which is available at http://www.gse.harvard.edu/~ngt.

14. Humphrey and Wechsler, "Initial Findings from a National Study," p. 483.

CHAPTER 5

BUT DO THEY STAY? ADDRESSING ISSUES OF TEACHER
RETENTION THROUGH ALTERNATIVE CERTIFICATION

Jason A. Grissom

1. Sheila N. Kirby, Linda Darling-Hammond, and Lisa Hudson, "Nontraditional Recruits to Mathematics and Science Teaching," *Educational Evaluation and Policy Analysis, 11*, No. 3 (1989): 301–323; Trish Stoddart, "An Alternative Route to Teacher Certification: Preliminary Findings from the Los Angeles Unified School District Intern program," *Peabody Journal of Education 67* (1992): 84–122; Jianping Shen, "Has the Alternative Certification Policy Materialized Its Promise? A Comparison between Traditionally and Alternatively Certified Teachers in Public Schools," *Educational Evaluation and Policy Analysis, 19*, No. 3 (1997): 276–283; Kenneth M. Zeichner and Ann K. Schulte, "What We Know and Don't Know from Peer-Reviewed Research about Alternative Teacher Certification Programs," *Journal of Teacher Education, 52*, No. 4 (2001): 266–282.

2. Robert W. Houston, Faith Marshall, and Teddy McDavid, "Problems of Traditionally Prepared and Alternatively Certified First Year Teachers," *Education and Urban Society, 26*, No. 1 (1993): 78–89; Gary Natriello and Karen Zumwalt, "Challenges to an Alternative Route for Teacher Education," in Ann Lieberman (Ed.), *The Changing Contexts of Teaching* (Chicago: University of Chicago Press, 1992), 59–78; Jianping Shen, "Has the Alternative Certification Policy Materialized Its Promise? A Comparison between Traditionally and Alternatively Certified Teachers in Public Schools"; Donald Boyd, Pam Grossman, Hamilton Lankford,

Susanna Loeb, and James Wyckoff, "How Changes in Entry Requirements Alter the Teacher Workforce and Affect Student Achievement," *Education Finance and Policy, 1*, No. 2 (2006): 176–216.

3. Linda Darling-Hammond and Barnett Berry, "Recruiting Teachers for the 21st Century: The Foundation for Educational Equity," *Journal of Negro Education, 68*, No. 3 (1999): 254–279.

4. Cassandra M. Guarino, Lucrecia Santibañez, and Glenn A. Daley, "Teacher Recruitment and Retention: A Review of the Recent Empirical Literature," *Review of Educational Research, 76*, No. 2 (2006): 173–208.

5. Donald Grissmer and Sheila Kirby, *Patterns of Attrition Among Indiana Teachers: 1965–1987* (Santa Monica, CA: Rand Corporation, 1992); Eric Hanushek, John Kain, and Steven Rivkin, "Why Public Schools Lose Teachers," *Journal of Human Resources, 39*, No. 2 (2004): 326–354; Jennifer Imazeki, "Teacher Salaries and Teacher Attrition," *Economics of Education Review, 24*, No. 4 (2004): 431–449; Susanna Loeb, Linda Darling-Hammond, and John Luczak, "How Teaching Conditions Predict Teacher Turnover in California Schools," *Peabody Journal of Education, 80*, No. 3 (2005): 44–70; Michael Podgursky, Ryan Monroe, and Donald Watson, "The Academic Quality of Public School Teachers: An Analysis of Entry and Exit Behavior," *Economics of Education Review, 23*, No. 5 (2004): 507–518; Todd Stinebrickner, "An Empirical Investigation of Teacher Attrition," *Economics of Education Review, 17*, No. 2 (1998): 127–136; Katherine O. Strunk and Joseph P. Robinson, "Oh, Won't You Stay: A Multilevel Analysis of the Difficulties in Retaining Qualified Teachers," *Peabody Journal of Education, 81*, No. 4 (2006): 65–94.

6. Donald Boyd, Hamilton Lankford, Susanna Loeb, and James Wyckoff, "Explaining the Short Careers of High-Achieving Teachers in Schools with Low-Performing Students," *American Economic Review, 95*, No. 2 (2005): 166–171; Hamilton Lankford, Susanna Loeb, and James Wyckoff, "Teacher Sorting and the Plight of Urban Schools: A Descriptive Analysis," *Educational Evaluation and Policy Analysis, 24*, No. 1 (2002): 37–62; Richard Murnane and Randall Olsen, "The Effect of Salaries and Opportunity Costs on Duration in Teaching: Evidence from Michigan," *Review of Economics and Statistics, 71*, No. 2 (1989): 347–352; Podgursky, Monroe, and Watson, "The Academic Quality of Public School Teachers: An Analysis of Entry and Exit Behavior."

7. Grissmer and Kirby, *Patterns of Attrition among Indiana Teachers: 1965–1987*; Murnane and Olsen, "The Effect of Salaries and Opportunity Costs on Duration in Teaching: Evidence from Michigan."

8. Strunk and Robinson, "Oh, Won't You Stay: A Multilevel Analysis of the Difficulties in Retaining Qualified Teachers."

9. Hanushek, Kain, and Rivkin, "Why Public Schools Lose Teachers"; Loeb, Darling-Hammond, and Luczak, "How Teaching Conditions Predict Teacher Turnover in California Schools"; Benjamin Scafidi, David Sjoquist, and Todd Stinebrickner, "Race, Poverty, and Teacher Mobility," *Economics of Education Review, 26*, No. 2 (2007): 145–159; Strunk and Robinson, "Oh, Won't You Stay: A Multilevel Analysis of the Difficulties in Retaining Qualified Teachers."

10. Loeb, Darling-Hammond, and Luczak, "How Teaching Conditions Predict Teacher Turnover in California Schools"; Strunk and Robinson, "Oh, Won't You Stay: A Multilevel Analysis of the Difficulties in Retaining Qualified Teachers."

11. Suzanne M. Wilson, Robert E. Floden, and Joan Ferrini-Mundy, *Teacher Preparation Research: Current Knowledge, Gaps, and Recommendations* (Seattle, WA: University of Washington, Center for the Study of Teaching and Policy, 2001), available online at http://depts.washington.edu/ctpmail/PDFs/TeacherPrep-WFFM-02-2001.pdf.

12. Guarino, Santibañez, and Daley, "Teacher Recruitment and Retention: A Review of the Recent Empirical Literature."

13. Michael Podgursky, "Research on Alternative Teacher Certification" (paper presented at the first annual conference of the National Center for Alternative Certification, San Antonio, Texas, February 1–3, 2004).

14. Guarino, Santibañez, and Daley, "Teacher Recruitment and Retention: A Review of the Recent Empirical Literature," p. 196.

15. Frank W. Lutz and Jerry B. Hutton, "Alternative Teacher Certification: Its Policy Implications for Classroom and Personnel Practice," *Educational Evaluation and Policy Analysis, 11*, No. 3 (1989): 237–254.

16. Michael B. Allen, *Eight Questions on Teacher Preparation: What Does the Research Say?* (Denver: Education Commission of the States, 2003).

17. Darling-Hammond and Berry, "Recruiting Teachers for the 21st Century: The Foundation for Educational Equity."

18. Edith Guyton, M. C. Fox, and Kathleen A. Sisk, "Comparison of Teaching Attitudes, Teacher Efficacy, and Teacher Performance of First Year Teachers Prepared by Alternative and Traditional Teacher Education Programs," *Action in Teacher Education, 13*, No. 2 (1991): 1–9.

19. Kirby, Darling-Hammond, and Hudson, "Nontraditional Recruits to Mathematics and Science Teaching."

20. Houston, Marshall, and McDavid, "Problems of Traditionally Prepared and Alternatively Certified First Year Teachers."

21. Natriello and Zumwalt, "Challenges to an Alternative Route for Teacher Education."

22. Margaret Raymond, Stephen Fletcher, and Javier Luque, *Teach For America: An Evaluation of Teacher Differences and Student Outcomes in Houston, Texas* (Palo Alto, CA: Stanford University, CREDO, 2001).

23. Shen, "Has the Alternative Certification Policy Materialized Its Promise? A Comparison between Traditionally and Alternatively Certified Teachers in Public Schools."

24. See, for rebuttal, Dale Ballou, "Alternative Certification: A Comment," *Educational Evaluation and Policy Analysis, 20*, No. 4 (1998): 313–315; Jianping Shen, "Alternative Certification: A Complicated Research Topic," *Educational Evaluation and Policy Analysis, 20*, No. 4 (1998): 316–319.

25. Boyd et al., "How Changes in Entry Requirements Alter the Teacher Workforce and Affect Student Achievement."

26. Zeichner and Schulte, "What We Know and Don't Know from Peer-Reviewed Research about Alternative Teacher Certification Programs."

27. Wilson, Floden, and Ferrini-Mundy, *Teacher Preparation Research: Current Knowledge, Gaps, and Recommendations.*

28. See, for example, Shawna Cox, Randall Parmer, Steven Tourkin, Toni Warner, and Deanna M. Lyter, *Documentation for the 2004–05 Teacher Follow-Up Survey*, NCES 2007-349 (U.S. Department of Education, Washington, DC: National Center for Education Statistics, 2007).

29. Shen, "Has the Alternative Certification Policy Materialized Its Promise? A Comparison between Traditionally and Alternatively Certified Teachers in Public Schools."

30. Dale Ballou, "Alternative Certification: A Comment," *Educational Evaluation and Policy Analysis, 20*, No. 4 (1998): 313–315.

31. Steven G. Rivkin, Eric A. Hanushek, and John F. Kain, "Teachers, Schools, and Academic Achievement," *Econometrica, 73*, No. 2 (2005): 417–458.

32. John Marvel, Deanna M. Lyter, Pia Peltola, Gregory A. Strizek, Beth A. Morton, and Renee Rowland, *Teacher Attrition and Mobility: Results from the 2004–05 Teacher Follow-Up Survey*, NCES 2007-307 (U.S. Department of Education, National Center for Education Statistics, Washington, DC: U.S. Government Printing Office, 2006).

33. Grissmer and Kirby, *Patterns of Attrition Among Indiana Teachers: 1965–1987*; Hanushek, Kain, and Rivkin, "Why Public Schools Lose Teachers"; Richard Murnane, Judith Singer, and John Willett, "Implications for Teacher Supply and Methodological Lessons for Research," *Educational Researcher, 17*, No. 6 (1988): 22–30.

34. Cox et al., *Documentation for the 2004–05 Teacher Follow-Up Survey.*

35. Zeichner and Schulte, "What We Know and Don't Know from Peer-Reviewed Research about Alternative Teacher Certification Programs."

CHAPTER 6

ASSESSING THE EFFECTIVENESS OF TEACHERS FROM DIFFERENT
PATHWAYS: ISSUES AND RESULTS

Marsha Ing and Susanna Loeb

1. National Center for Alternative Certification, *Alternative Routes to Teacher Certification: An Overview*, available online at http://www.teach-now.org/overview.html; U.S. Department of Education, *Alternative Routes to Teacher Certification* (Washington, DC: U.S. Department of Education, Office of Innovation and Improvement, 2004), available online at http://www.ed.gov/admins/tchrqual/recruit/altroutes/report.pdf.

2. Kenneth M. Zeichner and Hilary G. Conklin, "Teacher Education Programs," in Marilyn Cochran-Smith and Kenneth M. Zeichner (Eds.), *Studying Teacher Education*, (Mahwah, NJ: Lawrence Erlbaum, 2005), 645–735.

3. Daniel C. Humphrey and Marjorie E. Wechsler, "Insights into Alternative Certification: Initial Findings from a National Study," *Teachers College Record, 109*, No. 3 (2007): 483–530.

4. Zeichner and Conklin, "Teacher Education Programs."

5. See, for example, Linda Darling-Hammond, "Teacher Quality and Student Achievement: A Review of State Policy Evidence," *Education Policy Analysis Archives, 8*, No. 1 (2000), available online at http://epaa.asu.edu/epaa/v8n1/.

6. See, for example, Leonard Feldt and Robert Brennan, "Reliability," in Robert L. Linn (Ed.), *Educational Measurement*, 3rd ed. (New York: Macmillan, 1989), 105–146; Samuel Messick, "Validity," in Robert L. Linn (Ed.), *Educational Measurement*, 3rd ed. (New York: Macmillan, 1989), 13–103.

7. Robert Lissitz and Huynh Huynh, "Vertical Equating for State Assessments: Issues and Solutions in Determination of Adequate Yearly Progress and School Accountability," *Practical Assessment, Research & Evaluation, 8*, No. 1 (2003), available online at http://pareonline.net/getvn.asp?v=8&n=10.

8. Donald Boyd, Pam Grossman, Hamilton Lankford, Susanna Loeb, and James Wyckoff, "How Changes in Entry Requirements Alter the Teacher Workforce and Affect Student Achievement," *Education Finance and Policy, 1*, No. 2 (2006): 176–216.

9. Joan L. Herman and Noreen M. Webb, "Alignment Methodologies," *Applied Measurement in Education, 20*, No. 1 (2007): 1–5.

10. See, for example, American Educational Research Association, American Psychological Association, and National Council on Measurement in Education, *Standards for Educational and Psychological Testing* (Washington, DC: American Psychological Association, 1999).

11. See, for example, David R. Rogosa, "Statistical Misunderstandings of the Properties of School Scores and School Accountability," in Joan L. Herman and Edward H. Haertel (Eds.), *Uses and Misuses of Data for Educational Accountability and Improvement, National Society for the Study of Education, NSSE Yearbook, Vol. 104, Part 2* (Malden, MA: Blackwell Publishing, 2005), 147–174.

12. Lee S. Shulman, *Assessment of Teaching or Assessment for Teaching?* (paper prepared for the Educational Testing Service, San Francisco, CA, September 24–25, 2007), 5.

13. Paul T. Decker, Daniel P. Mayer, and Steven Glazerman, *The Effects of Teach For America on Students: Findings from a National Evaluation* (Princeton, NJ: Mathematica Policy Research, Inc., 2004).

14. Donald T. Campbell and Julian C. Stanley, *Experimental and Quasi-Experimental Designs for Research* (Chicago: Rand McNally, 1966); William R. Shadish, Thomas D. Cook, and Donald T. Campbell, *Experimental and Quasi-Experimental Designs for Generalized Causal Inference* (Boston: Houghton Mifflin, 2002).

15. Barbara Schneider, Martin Carnoy, Jeremy Kilpatrick, William H. Schmidt, and Richard J. Shavelson, *Estimating Causal Effects Using Experimental and Observational Designs* (Washington, DC: American Educational Research Association, 2007).

16. Campbell and Stanley, *Experimental and Quasi-Experimental Designs for Research*, p. 23.
17. See for reviews, Gerald W. Bracey, "Value-Added Models, Front and Center," *Phi Delta Kappan, 87*, No. 6 (2006): 716–717; Kilchan Choi, Pete Goldschmidt, and Kyo Yamashiro, "Exploring Models of School Performance: From Theory to Practice," in Joan L. Herman and Edward H. Haertel (Eds.), *Uses and Misuses of Data for Educational Accountability and Improvement, NSSE Yearbook, Vol. 104, Part 2* (Malden, MA: Blackwell Publishing, 2005), 119–146; Robert Lissitz (Ed.), *Value-Added Models in Education: Theory and Applications* (Maple Grove, MN: JAM Press, 2005); Daniel F. McCaffrey, Daniel M. Koretz, J. R. Lockwood, and Laura S. Hamilton, *Evaluating Value-Added Models for Teacher Accountability* (Santa Monica, CA: RAND, 2003); Robert Meyer, "Value-Added Indicators of School Performance: A Primer," *Economics of Education Review, 16*, No. 3 (1997): 183–301.
18. McCaffrey, Koretz, Lockwood, and Hamilton, *Evaluating Value-Added Models for Teacher Accountability*, p. 17.
19. Dale Ballou, William Sanders, and Paul Wright, "Controlling for Student Background in Value-Added Assessment of Teachers," *Journal of Educational and Behavioral Statistics, 29*, No. 1 (2004): 37–65; Daniel F. McCaffrey, J. R. Lockwood, Daniel M. Koretz, Thomas A. Louis, and Laura S. Hamilton, "Models for Value-Added Modeling of Teacher Effects," *Journal of Educational and Behavioral Statistics, 29*, No. 1 (2004): 139–144.
20. Teach For America, "In Strong Job Market, Record Number of Graduating Seniors Apply to Teach For America" (June 1, 2006), available online at http://www. teachforamerica.org/newsroom/documents/TeachForAmerica_news_20060601. html.
21. Decker, Mayer, and Glazerman, *The Effects of Teach For America on Students: Findings from a National Evaluation*.
22. Margaret Raymond, Stephen H. Fletcher, and Javier Luque, *Teach For America: An Evaluation of Teacher Differences and Student Outcomes in Houston, Texas* (Stanford, CA: The Hoover Institute, Center for Research on Education Outcomes [CREDO], 2001), available online at http://credo.stanford.edu/downloads/tfa. pdf.
23. Raymond, Fletcher, and Luque, *Teach For America: An Evaluation of Teacher Differences and Student Outcomes in Houston, Texas.*
24. Linda Darling-Hammond, Deborah J. Holtzman, Su Jin Gatlin, and Julian Vasquez Heilig, "Does Teacher Preparation Matter? Evidence about Teacher Certification, Teach For America and Teacher Effectiveness," *Education Policy Analysis Archives, 13*, No. 42 (2005), available online at http://epaa.asu.edu/epaa/ v13n42/.
25. Thomas J. Kane, Jonah E. Rockoff, and Douglas O. Staiger, "Photo Finish: Certification Doesn't Guarantee a Winner," *Education Next, 7*, No. 1 (2007): 61–67; Boyd, Grossman, Lankford, Loeb, and Wyckoff, "How Changes in Entry Requirements Alter the Teacher Workforce and Affect Student Achievement."

26. Zeyu Xu, Jane Hannaway, and Colin Taylor, "Making a Difference: The Effects of TFA in High Schools," CALDER Working Paper (Washington, DC, 2008).
27. Zeichner and Conklin, "Teacher Education Programs," p. 680.
28. Boyd, Grossman, Lankford, Loeb, and Wyckoff, "How Changes in Entry Requirements Alter the Teacher Workforce and Affect Student Achievement."
29. Pam Grossman, Karen Hammerness, Morva A. McDonald, and Matthew Ronfeldt, "Constructing Coherence: Structural Predictors of Perceptions of Coherence in NYC Teacher Education Programs," Teacher Policy Research Working Paper (Albany, NY: Teacher Policy Research, 2007).
30. Boyd, Grossman, Lankford, Loeb, and Wyckoff, "How Changes in Entry Requirements Alter the Teacher Workforce and Affect Student Achievement"; Kane, Rockoff, and Staiger, "Photo Finish: Certification Doesn't Guarantee a Winner."
31. Boyd, Grossman, Lankford, Loeb, and Wyckoff, "How Changes in Entry Requirements Alter the Teacher Workforce and Affect Student Achievement," p. 207.
32. John W. Miller, Michael C. McKenna, and Beverly A. McKenna, "A Comparison of Alternatively and Traditionally Prepared Teachers," Journal of Teacher Education, 49, No. 3 (1998): 165–176.
33. Boyd, Grossman, Lankford, Loeb, and Wyckoff, "How Changes in Entry Requirements Alter the Teacher Workforce and Affect Student Achievement"; Dan Goldhaber, "Everyone's Doing It, But What Does Teacher Testing Tell Us About Teacher Effectiveness," Journal of Human Resources, 42, No. 4: 765–794; Douglas N. Harris and Tim R. Sass, "Teacher Training and Teacher Productivity" (paper presented at the American Education Finance Association annual conference, New Orleans, LA, March 23–25, 2006).
34. Goldhaber, "Everyone's Doing It, But What Does Teacher Testing Tell Us about Teacher Effectiveness?"
35. Goldhaber, "Everyone's Doing It, But What Does Teacher Testing Tell Us about Teacher Effectiveness?"
36. Goldhaber, "Everyone's Doing It, But What Does Teacher Testing Tell Us about Teacher Effectiveness?"
37. Joshua D. Angrist and Jonathan Guryan, "Teacher Testing, Teacher Education, and Teacher Characteristics," The American Economic Review, 9, No. 2 (2004): 241–246; Drew Gitomer, Andrew S. Latham, and Robert Ziomek, The Academic Quality of Prospective Teachers: The Impact of Admissions and Licensure Testing (Princeton, NJ: Educational Testing Service, 1999).
38. Donald Boyd, Pam Grossman, Hamilton Lankford, Susanna Loeb, and James Wyckoff, "Teacher Preparation and Student Achievement" (paper presented at the annual Association for Public Policy Analysis and Management research conference, Washington, D.C., November 8–10, 2007).
39. Decker, Mayer, and Glazerman, The Effects of Teach For America on Students: Findings from a National Evaluation.
40. Miller, McKenna, and McKenna, "A Comparison of Alternatively and Traditionally Prepared Teachers."

41. Raymond Barclay, Emily Feistritzer, Richard Grip, Charlene Haar, Gregory Seaton, Sharon Sherman, and Meredith Stone, *The New Jersey Alternate Route Program: An Analysis of Perspectives from Alternate Route Teachers, Alternate Route Instructors, and Alternate Route Mentors* (2008), available online at http://www.state.nj.us/education/educators/license/research/alternate.pdf.

42. James Jelmberg, "College-Based Teacher Education versus State-Sponsored Alternative Programs," *Journal of Teacher Education, 47*, No. 1 (1996): 60–66.

43. U.S. Department of Education, *Alternative Routes to Teacher Certification.*

44. See, for example, Leigh Burstein, *Conceptual Considerations in Instructionally Sensitive Assessment*, CSE Technical Report 333 (Los Angeles, CA: Center for Research on Evaluation, Standards, and Student Testing, 1989); W. James Popham, "Determining the Instructional Sensitivity of Accountability Tests" (paper presented at the annual Large-Scale Assessment Conference, Council of Chief State School Officers, San Francisco, CA, June 25–28, 2006); Maria Araceli Ruiz-Primo, Richard J. Shavelson, Laura S. Hamilton, and Steve Klein, "On the Evaluation of Systematic Science Education Reform: Searching for Instructional Sensitivity," *Journal of Research in Science Teaching, 39*, No. 5 (2002): 369–393.

CONCLUSION
TAKING STOCK: FUTURE DIRECTIONS FOR PRACTICE AND RESEARCH
Pam Grossman and Susanna Loeb

1. See Donald Boyd, Pam Grossman, Hamilton Lankford, H., Susanna Loeb, and James Wyckoff, "How Changes in Entry Requirements Alter the Teacher Workforce and Affect Student Achievement," *Education Finance and Policy, 1*, No. 2 (2006).

2. "Teach For America Announces Record Number of Teachers for 2008," accessed online at www.teachforamerica.org/newsroom/documents/051408_Record_Corps.htm.

3. See Boyd et al., "How Changes in Entry Requirements Alter the Teacher Workforce."

4. See Marsha Ing and Susanna Loeb, this volume, for a review of this literature. See also Kenneth Zeichner and Hilary Conklin, "Teacher Education Programs," in Marilyn Cochran-Smith and Kenneth Zeichner (Eds.), *Studying Teacher Education* (Mahwah, NJ: Lawrence Erlbaum, 2005).

5. See Emily Feistritzer, *Alternative Teacher Certification: A State by State Analysis 2007* (Washington, DC: National Center for Educational Information, 2008) for a related effort to categorize programs by features rather than by labels. She includes eleven different classes of alternative-route programs, from those that are highly selective and unrestricted to those that are reserved for specific populations.

6. See Kate Walsh and Sandi Jacobs, "*Alternative Certification Isn't Alternative*," (Washington, DC: Thomas B. Fordham Institute and National Council on Teacher Quality, 2007).

7. See http://www.bpe.org/btr/ for a description of the Boston Residency Program.

8. See www.nycteachingfellows.org for an overview of the NYC Teaching Fellows Program. See also www.tntp.org for description of The New Teacher Project.

9. See http://www1.cuny.edu/academics/academic-programs/programs-of-note/teaching-opportunity-program/program-summary.html for more information on this program.

10. See Donald Boyd, Pam Grossman, Karen Hammerness, R. Hamilton Lankford, Susanna Loeb, Morva McDonald, Michelle Reininger, Matthew Ronfeldt, and James Wyckoff, "Surveying the Landscape of Teacher Education in New York City: Constrained Variation and the Challenge of Innovation," *Educational Analysis and Policy Analysis,* in press.

11. See Boyd et al., *Surveying the Landscape of Teacher Education in New York City;* See also Susan Moore Johnson and Sarah E. Birkeland (this volume) and Daniel C. Humphrey and Marjorie E. Wechsler (this volume).

12. See http://www.ausl-chicago.org/ourprogram/teachingresidency.htm for more information on this program.

13. See Raymond Barclay, Emily Feistritzer, Richard Grip, Charlene Haar, Gregory Seaton, Sharon Sherman, and Meredith Stone, *The New Jersey Alternate Route Program: An Analysis of the Perspectives from Alternate Route Teachers, Alternate Route Instructors, and Alternate Route Mentors,* downloaded from http://www.state.nj.us/education/educators/license/research/alternate.pdf, March 15, 2008.

14. See Boyd et al., 2008; Walsh and Jacobs, "*Alternative Certification Isn't Alternative.*"

15. See Donald Boyd, Pam Grossman, Hamilton Lankford, Susanna Loeb, and James Wyckoff, "Teacher Preparation and Student Achievement," Working Paper (Stanford, CA: Stanford University, February, 2008).

16. See Pam Grossman and Morva McDonald, "Back to the Future: Directions for Research in Teaching and Teacher Education," in *American Educational Research Journal 45,* No 1 (2008): 184–205, for a discussion of how to move toward a pedagogy of enactment in teacher preparation.

About the Contributors

Sarah E. Birkeland is a senior research associate at Education Matters in Cambridge, Massachusetts, and an affiliate of the Project on the Next Generation of Teachers at Harvard. A former elementary and middle school teacher, she studies teacher induction, leadership development, and continuous instructional improvement efforts. She is coauthor of *Finders and Keepers: Helping New Teachers Survive and Thrive in Our Schools.*

Jason A. Grissom is an assistant professor of public affairs at the Harry S Truman School of Public Affairs at the University of Missouri. His research spans education politics and policy analysis, school finance, and teacher labor markets. He holds an MA in education and a PhD in political economics from Stanford University.

Pam Grossman is a professor of education at Stanford University. Her research focuses on the relationship between policy and practice in the area of teacher education, adolescent literacy, and professional education. A former high school English teacher, Grossman teaches the prospective English teachers in Stanford's teacher-education program. Along with her colleagues Don Boyd, Hamilton Lankford, Susanna Loeb, and James Wyckoff, she has been engaged in a three-year study of pathways into teaching in New York City schools, focusing on the features of preparation that affect student achievement and teacher retention.

Karen Hammerness is a senior researcher with Stanford University. In the spring of 2007, she was a visiting professor at Leiden University in The Netherlands. Her research focuses upon teacher-preparation practices and policies, as well as teacher's ideals and visions. Her book, *Seeing through Teachers' Eyes: Professional Ideals and Classroom Practices*, was published last year by Teachers College Press.

Daniel C. Humphrey is the associate director for SRI International's Center for Education Policy. His research is focused on teacher policy and urban school reform. He currently leads studies of teacher induction in the Midwest, high school reform in Chicago, and district redesign in Austin, Texas. A former teacher and principal, Dr. Humphrey is a graduate of Teachers College, Columbia University.

Elizabeth A. Hutchinson is a doctoral candidate in curriculum and instruction at the University of Wisconsin-Madison. Her research focuses on beginning teacher induction and mentoring.

Marsha Ing is a postdoctoral fellow at the Stanford University School of Education's Institute for Research on Education Policy and Practice. She obtained a bachelor's degree in educational psychology from the University of Hawaii and an MA and PhD from the Social Research Methodology Division at the University of California, Los Angeles. Her research interests include methods for measuring and linking student performance and instructional opportunities, and increasing the instructional utility of student assessments.

Susan Moore Johnson is the Pforzheimer Professor of Teaching and Learning at the Harvard Graduate School of Education, where she served as the academic dean from 1993 to 1999. A former high school teacher and administrator, Johnson studies and teaches about teacher policy, school organization, educational leadership, and school improvement in schools and school systems. Johnson is director of the Project on the Next Generation of Teachers, which conducts research about how best to recruit, support, and retain a strong teaching force. She is coauthor of *Finders and Keepers: Helping New Teachers Survive and Thrive in Our Schools.*

Susanna Loeb is an associate professor of education at Stanford University and director of the Institute for Research on Education Policy and Practice. She specializes in the economics of education and the relationship between schools and federal, state, and local policies. She studies resource allocation, looking specifically at how teachers' preferences and teacher-preparation policies affect the distribution of teaching quality across schools, and how the structure of state finance systems affects the level and distribution of funds to districts. She also studies poverty policies, including welfare reform and early-childhood education programs. Susanna is an associate professor of business (by courtesy) at Stanford, a faculty research fellow at the National Bureau of Economic Research, and co-director of Policy Analysis for California Education.

Michelle Reininger is an assistant professor of Human Development and Social Policy and Learning Sciences and a faculty fellow at the Institute for Policy Research at Northwestern University. Her broad research agenda is aimed at gaining a better understanding of the dynamics of teacher and principal labor markets, including preparation, recruitment, and retention. She also studies how geography affects teachers' occupational decisionmaking; the role community colleges play in supplying teachers to areas with hard-to-staff schools; the importance of the student-teaching placement in teacher preparation; and the relationship between access to child care and teacher entry and exit behavior from the labor force. A former chemistry teacher, Dr. Reininger holds a PhD in the economics of education from Stanford University.

Marjorie E. Wechsler is a senior policy analyst for SRI International's Center for Education Policy. Much of her recent work has concentrated on teacher development throughout the teaching career, including preparation, induction, and continuing professional development. She currently leads studies of teacher professional development in Florida, teacher induction in the Midwest, and high school reform in Chicago. A former teacher, Dr. Wechsler is a graduate of Stanford University.

Kenneth Zeichner is the Hoefs-Bascom Professor of Teacher Education and associate dean, School of Education, University of Wisconsin-Madison. Zeichner's work focuses on teacher education, teacher professional development, and action research. He has published widely on these topics in North America, Europe, Latin America, and Australia. His books include *Democratic Teacher Education Reform in Africa: The Case of Namibia*; *Reflective Teaching*; *Currents of Reform in Pre-Service Teacher Education*; *Creating Equitable Classrooms through Classroom Action Research*; *Studying Teacher Education*; and *Teacher Education and the Struggle for Social Justice*. He is currently an editor of the international journal, *Educational Action Research*.

Index